THE ROCK & ROLL YEARS OF CHAS Before DAVE

Dedications

To my mother, Daisy.
Born 19 March 1913. Died 19 January 1984.

My thanks to John Pidgeon.
Without him I wouldn't have started this book.
Also, very special thanks to my wife Joan.
Without her I wouldn't have finished it.

THE ROCK & ROLL YEARS OF CHAS Before DAVE

Chas Hodges

Lennard Publishing
1987

First published 1987 by
Lennard Publishing, a Division of Lennard Books Ltd
The Old School, Brewhouse Hill,
Wheathampstead, Herts AL4 8AN

British Library Cataloguing in Publication Data
Hodges, Chas
The rock & roll years of Chas before Dave
1. Rock music – Great Britain – History
and criticism
I. Title
784.5′4′00924 ML3534

ISBN 1 85291 002 X

Editor Michael Leitch
Designed by Pocknell & Co
Photoset by Jigsaw Graphics
Printed in England

Contents

Foreword

We've just done a show and we're back at the hotel having a pint and a chat. We sit around for a while and I start to feel pretty knackered.

Chas says to me, 'I think I'll go up and do me book.' I think to meself, 'How can he get his brainbox working this time of night?' (It's three in the morning.) Maybe he wants to write something down before he forgets it. This is just one little instance I can recall when Chas was puttin' this together and I for one am really glad he did go up and 'do his book'.

There's tales in these pages even I hadn't heard before. It's all in here, my mate's account from when he was a nipper in Edmonton, right up until the time he got tangled up with me.

Have a butchers. I bet you'll enjoy reading it as much as I did.

Dave Peacock
(The Other Half)

TEA

Introduction

Why are you reading this Introduction? I never do! If I've bought a book about somebody I like I wanna get straight into the story to find out what sort of things he got up to and what makes him tick.

But perhaps you ain't bought it yet and you're reading this bit in the shop in hopes it'll give you an idea of what it's all about and if it's worth spending your money on? I'll tell ya one thing. It's got a few swear words in it. But you see, that's the way I talk! I use 'em like perfect punctuation. You don't notice them. But you would if they weren't there. The same as if you had no full stops or commas, the words would be there but the flow and rhythm would be lost. Now I might slip up on me full stops and commas here and there, but I do know where to put a swear word!

What else is this book about? It ain't all swearing, is it? Sod that! (Know what I mean!) What about the entertainment and interest value? What's he goin' on about in all them pages? Has he just put a lot of words down to please the publisher just so's the book looks thick, then once it's bought who cares 'cos you've already paid your money and it don't matter if you don't like it and don't buy any more of his books 'cos he's not doin' any more anyway? (Phew!) Well, listen here ol' chum, if *that's* what you think, you haven't got a very high opinion of *me*, have you? Took me four bloody years to write this book. If I wasn't bothered about what went in it, I'd have had it done in a week! So that's enough of that!

So, what's it about then? It's about my life up until I got together with Dave. The school days. The early Rock 'n' Roll days. The Fifties. London street life. The serious bits. The funny bits. The days spent on the road with mad but likeable blokes like Gene Vincent and Jerry Lee Lewis. The laughing and learning. The Soul Scene in the Sixties with Cliff Bennett and The Rebel Rousers. Touring with The Beatles. The daft but exciting American tours in the Seventies with Heads Hands and Feet. The skint and the rich times. The hit records and the flops. The wonderful and the wallies. In short, the bits you look back on as all part of growing up.

I hope you do enjoy this book 'cos one day, when I am grown up, I might write another one.

Chapter 1

First Memories

I'm Chas, the one who plays the piano in Chas 'n' Dave. I was born in the North Middlesex Hospital, Edmonton on the 28th December, 1943. Albert and Daisy Hodges were the 'proud' parents (so my Mum tells me, and I believe everything my Mum says!). Brother Dave was nearly three years old. Mum wanted me to be called Nicholas but Charles was the traditional family name on my Dad's side. So I became Charles Nicholas. 'Chas' was also the familiar nickname for Charles around Hackney, where my Dad came from, so 'Chas' I was called.

My earliest memories were when I was about three. Music amongst the most vivid of 'em.

My Dad was a lorry driver and worked for an Italian named Romano. Romano owned a farmhouse in Ashford, Kent, that was 'to let' and Dad decided that we should move down there. Edmonton was alright, where we were living with my Mum's Mum and Dad, but he wanted something better for us. We moved to Kent in the summer of 1947. It was good down there: I loved it. Considering I was only young and we were only there for about six months, I have a lot of vivid memories about the time.

The journey down in my Dad's old green van. Me asking Dad if it was putting your hands on the steering wheel that made it move along. Dad taking his hands off the steering wheel while we were going along to prove that it wasn't. I was impressed. The arrival at the farm. Being met by Ginger, the farm hand, who never lifted a finger, let alone a hand!

Dad at the top of an apple tree slinging apples down to my Uncle Bert.

Waking in the morning to see the hunt go by. I thought it was a magnificent sight.

Stella our Alsatian. Peggy and Spike the greyhounds.

Collecting new laid eggs and being chased by one of the cockerels. Was I frightened! He was nearly as big as me! I injured my finger slamming the door of the run and I remember Mum making me sit quiet with my finger in a glass of TCP.

Dad wringing the cockerel's neck in case he pecked us kids' eyes out. Me getting chased again by the cockerel! (We had 2 cockerels. A wild one and a tame one. Dad had wrung the wrong one's neck.)

Garlic in my Wellingtons. (An idea of Mum's to keep the colds away.)

The pond in the woods that had Witches. (Another idea of Mum's to stop us kids going near it.) New discoveries like oak apples, mole hills, cowpats, straw. Brother Dave chucking some 12-bore cartridges behind the Rayburn stove and Mum going mad even though Dave kept insisting that it didn't matter 'cos they were dead ones. Dad coming home with a rabbit for dinner. Spitting out the lead shot. The smell of Dad's van in the garage. Carbon monoxide even now brings back happy memories! Me and my brother and Stella the Alsatian playing in the haystack. 'Housewives Choice' on the radio.

Songs like 'Cruising down the River' – a popular song I liked. I told my brother, 'That's *my* song!'. 'No it's not, it's the lady on the radio's.' Little git.

'Feniculee Fenicula'. 'The Thieving Magpie'.

I'd watch magpies from my bedroom window with that tune going through my head. One day we had company. My Mum announced them to me and my brother as being 'off the stage'. I remember standing in this sunny room as the couple went into their act. The lady played the piano and the man sang.

Top The back yard at Harton Road. I reckon about 1937. Left to right: Mum and boyfriend (Bill Buckler), Aunt Lil, Dad (before he chatted up Mum, not looking very happy!), Aunt Maggie, Nan and Uncle Alf. **Above** Mum and Dad (after he had chatted up Mum and looking very happy!).

Above Mum and Dad on Southend Pier in 1939. **Right** Mum and 'Big' brother Dave, 1940. **Below** Dad in his football team. Dad is second from the right. You can just see the fag hanging out of his mouth if you look close. I don't know if he put it out when he was playing. Football was different in those days!

The song was 'Blue Room'. They were a bit on the posh side but they were quite good at what they did. (I had 'em sussed although I was only three.)

It was a good memory. It was music.

Grown-ups always looked happy when they were singing. Especially when someone was playing the piano. Why didn't they do this *all* the time?

I have fond memories of that place. I loved it. It was where my Dad *lived*. When I think of him walking about, or drinking a cup of tea, or working on his old van, it was all down in Kent. I didn't remember him before that. I was too young. My Mum doesn't have the same affection for the place. But it was different for Mum. To her it was where my Dad *died*. The day before my fourth birthday my Dad died of wounds from a 12-bore shotgun. I remember it happening but I was too young to take it in. Not see him again?

Dead? No! All dead people died before I was born.

It was his own hand that fired the gun. Nobody knew why.

We left the farm before the New Year and came back to Edmonton to live with my Nan, Grandad and Great-grandfather.

Chapter 2

11, Harton Road

Us kids, like kids do, adapted quickly once more to North London life. Mum earnt extra money to keep us by playing piano up the 'Ex' (the Exhibition pub on Edmonton Green). Nan and Grandad helped bring us up while Great-grandfather Shaw, who was nearly 90 years old then, sort of acted the part of comic relief. He was a good old boy, 5 foot 4 inches tall and full of life.

He lived in the boxroom which had a smell of old stale pipes which I quite liked. He was music mad. He played clarinet in his younger days and would go out busking with my Mum on harmonium. I never heard him play clarinet, although he was supposed to have been quite good. I only heard him play the whistle which he played day and night, whatever the hour. I'd get private recitals in his room. He'd show me the scales, or play his latest piece that had just come through the door from Keith Prowse. Grandfather would be off, stopping every now and again to repeat a passage he felt needed improvement.

I loved every minute. When it was time for a break, he'd light up his ol' pipe and go into a story. Most times it would be about music. A brass band he'd seen years ago. He'd describe all the sounds and what they played. I could hear that band as clearly as if I'd been there. Then he'd ask me what I was up to, what new toys had I got? 'New toy car? Lets have a look.' I'd go and get it. Grandfather would inspect it with wonder. Try it out with glee! Sometimes I'd say, 'You can borrow it for a while if you want, Grandfather.' 'Thanks boy. Thanks very much. I'll take care of it.'

He didn't get on with his son-in-law too well, though (Mum's Dad).

There was a thing in my house that was as important as the teapot or the gas stove or whatever was a household necessity.

It was the piss-pail.

He had one in his room. Nan and Grandad had one and me and my brother had one. We never had china piss-pots, too posh and didn't hold enough. We had galvanised piss-pails. Great-grandfather and Grandad would argue never-ending over who'd got whose piss-pail.

'You've got my piss-pail.'

'No I ain't, you silly old bastard!'

'Daisy!' Grandfather would shout to his daughter (Daisy was my Nan's name, too). 'Tell your husband he's got my piss-pail!' And so it would go on.

We kids had a white enamel piss-pail. It had a lid with holes on it. You could use it without taking the lid off, although I never owned up. My brother used to suss it when the lid felt warm, and I'd get a clump. I couldn't see the sense in takin' the lid off, as it all went in anyway. Short cuts to get the same results always appealed to me.

The nearest school to me was Eldon Road School. I started there shortly after I was four years old. My brother Dave, nearly three years older than me, was already at the school, and I couldn't wait to get there too. I begged my Mum to get me there as soon as possible. It must have been the glamour of it, big brother and all that, goin' off to school with all the lads. The morning I started I did just that. Went to school with all the lads. Now big brother, who was supposed to be lookin' after me, decided before we got close to Eldon Road that I was a bit of a nuisance and I was left to fend for myself. I'd got this Victoria plum my Mum had given me to take to school, and I decided to sit down against this wall outside the school gates to eat it. Some ol' gels (who were jawing on their front door steps) every now and then looked over at me. 'They've gone in, yer know,' they'd say, and then get back to their jawing. I never took no notice and carried on eating me plum.

To me the novelty had gone. I'd bin to school with the boys but I didn't want to go *in*, and that was that. Sitting up against the wall eating my Victoria plum and thinking about goin' to school was heaven. Goin' to school was great, but now I'd been. Now I wanted to go home, and I did. Those questions about 'Do you like goin' to school?' made sense. I did. I liked comin' home from school too. But *goin' in* to school was a different matter. Do you want to *go* to school? – that was all I was asked.

My Mum decided I wasn't ready to attend school and I was kept home 'til I was five. Try again.

I wasn't mad on it though I got to like it. When I started goin' to Eldon (and I was goin' *in* as well) I thought it was alright. Some teachers I didn't like, some I liked. My first teacher was an old gel named Miss Dames. One day she was teaching us a poem about a 'Teeny Tiny Key' - 'I know a little cupboard with a teeny, tiny key, and in there are cakes for me, me, me.' I can't remember the rest. We all had to recite this poem together. As the class was reciting I remember feeling a pain in my stomach, something I'd probably ate, and, I shit myself. It crept round my trousers all sort of warm. It wasn't lumpy and none dropped out, so I thought I'd be able to keep it a secret till I got home. It was four o'clock and the bell went at five past four. Now whether I had a funny look on my face or just chance I don't know, but Miss Dames said:

'Now before we all go home, children, Charles Hodges will come out and recite the poem to you all on his own.' I went out all soaked in shit, but it clung there, not showing itself as I went into 'I know a little cupboard with a teeny, tiny key.' I did it all through, word perfect. The bell went and I was off home. I run indoors and all I could say was, 'I couldn't help it, I couldn't help it!'

'What couldn't you help?' said Mum. 'What's the matter? Tell me, tell me!'

The 'couldn't help it' bit came about 'cos I'd gone home from school once laughing about a school mate who'd been in the same predicament. 'Ahh, he probably couldn't help it,' Mum had said, and I had latched onto that.

So after a bit she found out (it didn't take long!) that I'd shit myself. My Nan promptly took my trousers and pants off and put me outside on the toilet. What's she done that for? I thought. I've already done it! I sat there crying on the bog-hole. I'll never laugh at my mates again. It could well have been apples. Too many of 'em. I was mad on apples.

One day Mum and Nan decided to take me and my brother to Southend for the day. Grandad said, 'Take this bag of apples with yer, give some to the kids and give the rest away when you get down to Southend.'

It wasn't a bag, it was a sackfull! We had to catch the train at Lower Edmonton station, but the train was late. Me and my brother played up and down the station and I nicked an apple every time I got near the sack. Finally the train came along (the sack half empty by now) and off we went.

As we neared Southend, a thunderstorm started and, on top of that, so did one in my belly. Mum told my brother to take me to the toilet. He did, reluctantly. Boy, did I have the shits! My belly was aching like hell. I really thought I was gonna die. My brother Dave reported back to me Mum and then forgot what

The Shaw line, where I got my music from. Great–great–grandfather Samuel Shaw (left), Great grandfather William Shaw (right) and Nan (Daisy Tyler, née Shaw) with baby Mum. Funnily enough Dave Peacock is related to the Shaws. We've often wondered if we're distant relations.

Above A typical party in the front room at Harton Road (about 1935). Grandad Tyler (Mum's dad) has enjoyed himself – notice the hand up the ol' bird's skirt. Her ol' man looks none too pleased! **Below left** Nan and Uncle Alf. About the same period. **Below right** Much later. Aunt Lil, Grandad Tyler (sober) and Nan at St Osyth.

Above Canvey Island, 1953. Uncle Alf, Grandad Tyler, Aunt Maggie, Nan, Aunt Mary, Cousin Brian and me. I hated this picture, I thought I looked like a nutter. **Right** Uncle Alf, Nan, brother Dave and little me. I hated that hat too! **Below** Nan on an outing, sixth from the left next to Aunt Flo. Notice the beer bottles on the table. No posh white wine in those days.

toilet he'd put me in. I could hear him shouting 'Chas!' underneath the toilet doors miles away. I was answering feebly. He found me in the end. When I recovered we spent the rest of the day under a shelter away from the storm. But that wasn't all. I got me fingers shut in the train door on the way home! I've still got the scars to prove it. Some yobs, running down the platform, slammed our carriage door shut and my fingers were in the hinges. Nan sorted them out though, and gave their earholes a walloping to go home with.

Now you'd think from that first experience I'd hate the place. But I grew to love it. A trip to Southend was second only to Christmas Day. My favourite pastime down Southend was crabbing, in the boating pool. A bit of string with a piece of cockle or mussel tied to the other end, drop it in the pool, wait for a tug, and slowly pull it up. Sure enough there'd be a crab. Years later when I took my own kids down Southend I tried the same thing in the same pool (the one near the pier). I got the same results. Kids watching at first thought I was mad. Crabs in the boating pool? But they were away after bits of string and cockles and mussels before you knew it! Try it yourself, when you're next down Southend.

Harton Road was a typical London street of terraced houses. Our front garden was about 10 foot long by 3 foot wide with evergreens. Downstairs was the front room (most people didn't use theirs and kept it as 'best' but we had to use ours); the kitchen (with the old black leaded stove); scullery, or 'washus' as it was called; back yard about 30 foot long by 20 foot wide, outside toilet and old dug-up Anderson shelter at the end, which became Grandad's shed. There were three rooms upstairs and 11 stairs. I know, I counted 'em 'cos my ambition at the time was to jump all 11 stairs in one go.

I worked my way up, first one, then two, etc., until the day came to attempt the lot. I'd done 10 stairs, one more to go. My Nan would shout, 'You'll jump your legs in.' I never knew what she was talking about but I presumed she meant I'd end up a midget. I remember poising myself at the very top, waiting for the right moment (like a footballer does when he's taking an important penalty) to do what I had to do. It came. I took a flyin' leap, eyes fixed on the landing strip (the passage floor). I would have done it too if it hadn't been for the floor of the upstairs landing. I had to jump that bit higher to make the 11 stairs. Whack! My head hit the landing floor that jutted out above me, and I landed in a crumpled heap at the foot of the stairs. I never attempted it again. I stuck at 10.

The characters down our road were unique. Next door to us lived a gypsy family, who had mad kids. They had bows and arrows with real dart-heads screwed onto the arrows. They let their little sisters out of upstairs windows, cowboy-style, with ropes tied round their middles and all that. If you went in for a cup o' tea, you'd get it in a jam jar. Which, I gotta be honest, seemed a good idea. Why buy cups when you get jam jars for nothing? Though jam jars were handy too, when the roundabout man came round. For a jam jar you could get a ride on the roundabout. It was a small round wooden thing with sticks sticking out that the big kids grabbed hold of and pushed. The roundabout whizzed round full of little kids. It was a horrible sensation. We'd all get off feeling sick. But it was an occasion. This red, white, blue and green wooden roundabout thing turning up at the end of the street. Well, you had to have a go!

Mrs Barlow lived the other side. I played John Bunyan in the school play

Class of 1951, Eldon Road Juniors. Can you spot me? My mate Johnny Hitchens is on the left in the top row. I'm seventh from the left in the second row.

once and she lent me her long drawers. I played the part with, I thought, the dignity which it deserved. I couldn't make out why everyone was laughin'.

A woman who lived down the road *really* was mad. She was always on about spacemen and Mars and that. My Great-grandfather didn't know about this 'cos he was as deaf as a post. I remember one conversation I overheard that went, 'Where you goin' for your holidays?' Woman, 'I'm goin' to Mars.' Grandfather, 'I don't like them seaside places.'

Not everybody was mad in Harton Road though. Well, if you class being mad on music as bein' mad then perhaps a lot of 'em were. Music played a big part in our household. Mum played the piano which she taught herself, with the aid of Nan who had a great ear for music. 'Get your vamps right,' she'd say.

She wasn't interested in the twiddly bits up the top, like most self-taught pianists played, with anything for the left hand. With her the chords had to be right. She had the right idea. Mum learnt the hard way by just sloggin' at it till it *was* right. She had no teacher who knew how to play, only Nan who knew when it was wrong. Mum ended up with a unique style that is admired by many. Me included. I could never figure out her chord shapes or exactly what she was doin' but it sounded great.

Nan did play a bit of mouth organ though. She was a great critic too. Later on when I began to make records she always had something constructive to say and would come out with good ideas. Grandad (Mum's Dad) was the only unmusical one. He'd just sit back with his pint and enjoy the racket. He did sing now and again though. I learnt 'Not me' from Grandad, which we put on our first 'Jamboree Bag' album.

Grandad took over when Dad died. He was great, he loved an outing. Southend for the day, fishin' off the pier or just fishin' in the Lea down at

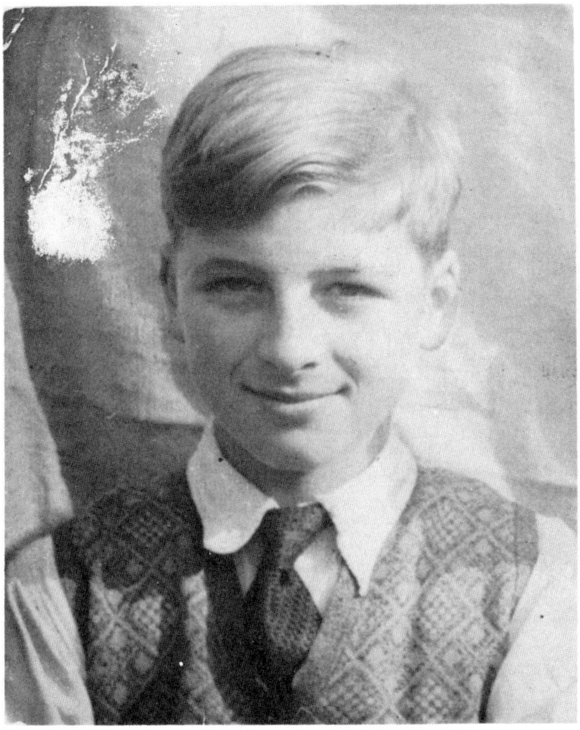

First year at Higher Grade school (aged 11).

Broxbourne. Grandad enjoyed it as much as us kids.

Mum often said to me at the time, 'Why don't you take up the piano? You've got a good ear.' But I didn't want to know. I loved music but I also loved fishing and football, and playing in the street. It wasn't until the guitar became popular that I wanted to play. But that was later. There was too much goin' on at the time for me to actually sit down and learn to play an instrument. My every spare moment was spent in the open air. If I wasn't over the Lea fishing or just messing about I was out in the street playin' games like 'runouts', 'end to the football', or 'Jimmy Knacker'.

Around 1953 when I was nearly ten I remember there were two gangs down our street. There was Kenny Stacey's gang with Bobby Cook as his right-hand man. In our book they were the trouble-makers. The other gang was led by my brother Dave with me as his right-hand man (at least *I* thought so!). We were the peacemakers, but ready to fight for peace! Kenny Stacey, a couple of years older than my brother, was talked about as being the best fighter in the street. When he spoke, everybody jumped, but not us. 'My brother could beat him any day,' I'd pipe up. 'Oh Yer?' would say his gang. 'Yer,' I'd say. And so on.

Now one day, me, me brother and our gang were out in the street playin' a game like 'Kingy' or something. Anyway, Kenny Stacey and his mob decided they'd join in, uninvited. Dave and Kenny Stacey got into an argument that developed into a fight that we all knew was inevitable sooner or later. Not only us kids but the grown-ups knew about the rivalry. One by one they came out of their front doors to watch the fight. They weren't about to stop it. They knew it had to happen. Soon almost the whole of the street were out watching. Nobody cheered or booed or nothing. They were there to witness a fair fight. Which it was. It seemed to go on for hours though it probably lasted more like about an hour. They fought from one end of the street to the other. Finally Kenny Stacey held up his hands. He was beaten. Brother Dave was champ!

From that day on I'd have no talk about Kenny Stacey being the Best Fighter in the Street. I had proof and so did the rest. Bobby Cook, though, never let up. Now my brother had sorted out Kenny Stacey, I decided itwas my duty to sort out Bobby Cook. As I have said, I was 10 and Bobby Cook was about 13, although we were roughly the same size. But Bobby Cook had a temper and when he lost it he *really* lost it!

I can't remember how it started, but shortly after my brother's fight with Kenny Stacey, me and Bobby Cook got into a scuffle in the street. He was stronger than me so *I* wasn't gonna let the fight go on for hours. I knew I'd get beat. We were in a clinch in the middle of the road and I was going under. I reached out in desperation more than anything and my hand fell upon half a house-brick. Wallop! I hit him right on top of the head with it. He went mad and I mean *mad!* I was up and running and he was close behind me screamin' with rage! I had half the length of the road to run to reach my front door. I glanced behind to see Bobby Cook grab a school railing that we'd been playing javelin throwing with. He meant business so I hoped and prayed that the 'string' was in the door. This string came through a hole in the front door and was attached to the lock. A quick pull and the front door was open. It was! I grabbed the string, was in like a shot and slammed the door just in time. The school railing that was meant for me ended up embedded in the front door! Thank gawd the string was in.

The four of us got on alright together after that.

There was always something going on in that street. If it wasn't a fight, it was a party (they liked excitement). Anybody who played an instrument down the street was well respected and sought after on such occasions. Mum was the best piano player down the street. If you got 'Daisy' to play piano at your party you knew it was gonna be a good one. Mum in fact was the best piano player for miles around. Everyone knew Daisy in and around Edmonton. The street was proud of her.

Music played a big part in that road. Johnny Wright (who taught me a few chords later on) played banjo. He still comes to see us now and is a good friend. There was Bob Weston over the road who played guitar, and his brother Tony. Before I started playin' people down the street would say to me, 'What do you play?' I didn't play anything! They were amazed. They knew about me Mum, Nan and Great-Grandfather. 'You ought to, then,' they'd say. Perhaps the combination of my family's and the street's encouragement got me goin'. Who knows? It must have helped.

Coronation Day was a great occasion. Everybody did their bit only too willingly. A real excuse for a party! Let's go! A stage was built outside Huffys, the local shop. A piano was got from somewhere, beer arrived like magic and away they went. Every night for a week the whole street had a great time. I enjoyed every minute of it. The grown-ups looked happy and we kids stayed up late.

'You love music,' Mum would say. 'Why don't you learn to play something?' But life was too full up for me to take time out to sit down and learn to play an instrument. My hours and weeks and months were crowded. If I wasn't fishing down Picketts Lock I'd be train spotting or goin' up the Spurs with my brother, or playing football wishin' I was as good as my brother. He played for Edmonton. Too much was goin' on.

About that time, Great-grandfather married his sixth wife, who left him a week later. Him and his mate 'Scally' (they were both in their nineties) met two birds and decided they would get married. They did, and both moved up to Grimsby. A week later, Great-grandfather arrived back at 11, Harton Road with a bag of dirty washing.

'She's thrown me out, Daisy,' he said to Nan. Great-grandfather was back in the fold. 'She wouldn't wash my dirty pants,' he said, and that was that. Scally came home shortly after. He'd got thrown out too. I remember Grandfather and Scally discussing their wives in Grandfather's room. Both of them were as deaf as posts. Entertaining!

In the meantime Mum married her second husband. Larry.

I wasn't mad on him. He didn't fit in. He didn't last either, and buggered off leaving Mum pregnant. 'The only good thing he ever done,' said Mum. She wanted a daughter and she had one. My half-sister Jean. My Mum's next husband was Irish John. She met him at the 'Ex'. I was 11.

Chapter 3
Irish John

The upset of Mum's last marriage had mellowed with time and contentment reigned. Life at home was good. Me, Mum, brother and sister lived upstairs. Great-grandfather in the box room, and Nan and Grandad lived downstairs. We all got on well together (after a fashion) and I was looking forward to starting my new school.

I'd scraped through the 11-plus and was going to Higher Grade, Edmonton. Halcyon days! But them Halcyon days were about to change, especially Sundays. Y'see, Mum married Irish John, and what used to be 'sitting round the ol' coal fire of a Sunday with a cup of tea, the pleasant wintery sun shining through the window and just the sound of the old clock ticking on the mantlepiece'. Sundays soon became 'a room full of Irishmen drinking whiskey, farting, and playing poker'.

Actually John wasn't a bad bloke really. He was as silly as arseholes when he was pissed, which was a good part of the time. I think my Mum didn't really mind him getting pissed though, 'cos he would make her laugh.

One day Mum was getting ready to go up the Green, shopping.

'Oi'll get your fluten shopping for ye,' says John, 'Oi'm going up the fluten green anyway.'

We never saw him 'til next day.

John's recollection of what happened was somewhat sketchy, to say the least, but between bits pieced together from acquaintances and policemen, the story went something like this.

John got the shopping. Then decides he'll go in the 'Ex' for a quick one before going home. John's 'quick one' ends up being longer than he originally planned. Before he knows what's happened, its two o'clock in the morning!

On the way home (he vaguely remembers this bit), he's realised he's left the shopping in the pub. It's foggy and he's pissed. It's a long way back to the pub, but he's been gone for over half a day and he ain't even coming home with the shopping. Dais' is gonna be none too pleased. But then he sees something (as though it were heaven sent!) that not only solves his problem, but will put him in Daisy's good books for evermore.

Through the mist he sees a lorry. The back is open and inside he sees something white. It looks like something that women like to buy for their kitchens. A fridge or a washing machine. He's dived in, nicked it and took it home on his shoulder for Dais'. He arrives home, puts it down on the door step to find his key, and then decides to have a look at what he's nicked. It turns out to be a washing machine. They had one in the digs where he used to stay. But didn't the big hole in the top use to have a lid on it? Where's the lid? He'd only forgotten the lid. Dais' will want a lid on it. He remembered seeing a round white bit in the back of that lorry. He must go back for the lid. He did. But so as not to spoil the surprise in case Daisy came out, he took the washing machine with him.

An hour later he arrives back at the scene of the crime. The lorry was still there. The back was still open. The lid was still there.

John went in after it.

Now, as it happened, the fog had begun to clear, and it turned out the lorry was parked outside Edmonton Police Station.

As John emerged from the lorry with the lid, he was spotted. John just heard 'Oi!' and ran with the washing machine and lid down the road. The coppers gave chase. John run in and out of turnings trying to sidetrack 'em but the boots behind him were getting closer. As a last resort, he slung the washing machine over his head into their path. Some of the boots stopped but a couple dodged out the way and finally caught up with him.

That was the first we heard. We got a 'phone call at four in the morning saying it was the police and they'd got Mr John Rice in their custody.

The headline in the local paper was, 'MAN THROWS MANGLE AT POLICEMAN'.

He got off light. He was fined £68, which his brother Packy paid.

Mum never sent him shopping no more.

Chapter 4
Schooldays and Rock 'n' Roll

Looking back, I had two sorts of mates at school. Almost complete opposites. Perhaps this reflects the different directions I was torn between. One of my mates, Johnny Hitchens, was a smashing fellow and I thought the world of him. We went up the Spurs together, we went fishing together, but he always did his homework and I didn't. I was always late for school but he wasn't. I admired him for this but instead of modelling myself on him, I accepted the fact that we were different in these respects and went my own way. I saw him not long ago for the first time since we left school. Me and Dave opened a fete at Eldon Road School and Johnny Hitchens turned up. He's now a teacher and I bet he's a good one too.

My other sort of mates were the ones that were just a little bit more daring than I was. I admired them too. I enjoyed their company. It was exciting. For instance, one of my mates, Tony Webster, was another fishing companion. We used to go camping together over at Cheshunt. One day I hit on the idea (to get our camp fire going better) that we go along the railway lines collecting bits of coal that had fallen from the trains. We spent a couple of hours doing this and came back with half a sack of coal. We had a good camp fire that night and decided we'd go back and collect some more coal the next day. But here comes the difference between him and me. I didn't mind wandering along the lines picking up stray bits of coal, but it wasn't quick enough for him. He's spotted a coal yard and he's over the fence.

'There's fuckin' loads of it over here!' I've heard, and then he's back with two sacks full. In my mind collecting coal from the trackside wasn't stealing so it was accceptable, but in Tony's mind we were collecting coal and the quicker you got it the better, no matter how. I sort of felt it wasn't quite right, but I liked his initiative.

Our camp fire for the rest of the week outshone everybody else's. It was the talk of the camp site. So much so the camp site bailiff came down to see us.

'Where did you get that coal from?' he said. We told him we got it from along the railway lines.

'Well you'd better bring it up to my house 'cos you're not supposed to have it.'

I felt we'd been found out and it was the only thing to do, but not Tony.

'Bollocks!' he said to me after the bailiff had gone. 'He only wants it for his own fire!'

'You're right,' I thought, and although I had a nagging feeling that it belonged more to the coal yard than to us, it was still more ours than *his*. (There's a moral in this somewhere, but I can't figure it out at the minute.)

As I began my new school at Higher Grade, the Rock 'n' Roll era was beginning and I was about to be hooked.

Although, at first, I didn't like it. All the kids were going mad on this bloke called Bill Haley. I couldn't see it. He was okay but he was not as good as Tennessee Ernie or Kay Starr or the boogie-woogie piano players I'd heard. But I hadn't heard Little Richard, or Jerry Lee then. Little did I know what I was in for!

I became a bit of an 'erbert at that school. Nobody got the cane more than me, nobody had longer hair than me. I suppose I was a bit cheeky sometimes, but even though I say it myself I was never nasty and I think most of the teachers liked me. I didn't mind the cane if I knew I was guilty, but I wouldn't accept it if I wasn't.

The Headmaster was a bastard. If you got sent to him you knew you were gonna be caned on the arse and that wasn't pleasant. It wasn't so much the pain. The worst part was the sick feeling you felt a few minutes after. Outside his study was a painting of a boy with a rabbit. That was all you had to look at as you was waiting to see the head who you knew was going to cane you. I've seen that picture since and the same feeling came over me. I wanted to go and have a shit. The poor sod who painted it never meant it to give off *that* feeling, I'm sure! The Headmaster loved caning kids. I'd look thru' my legs at the old bastard as he bent the cane about before he laid into you. He'd hardly listen to what you had to say for yourself. He didn't want to in case there might be a reason for letting you off. I was a 'bounder' and a 'thug' and had to be dealt with accordingly. I wasn't sure what 'bounder' meant although it didn't sound too bad, but I objected to being called a thug for kickin' a football thru' the school window. We used to make up stories of him and the Headmistress having a 'do' at playtime. With her whackin' him on the arse for a change.

Brother Dave on his motorbike down Harton Road. Must have been close to the Sixties 'cos cars started to appear down the street. The street is still there today but you can't see the kerb for cars.

'C'mon you lily whites!' I wasn't me in this team photo, I was Ted Ditchburn. Back, left to right: Kevin Knowler, Alec Hatch, Ray Holt, 'Ted Ditchburn', Alan Watkins, George Wilson. Sitting: Michael Verdon, Rodney Clarke, Ray Ketteridge, Jeff Clark, Keith Chambers.

The crafty fag smokin' sessions round the back of the bike sheds was an enlightening experience. We'd talk about who you was going to 'tit up' on the field and who you would like to 'tit up'. We used to have a PT teacher with big tits. She also taught us English (I think, I dunno, I couldn't think of anything else but tits). She'd come into class with her PT shorts on. If you played up, you were made to come and sit next to her. So I played up. I remember once havin' to sit at her desk while she sat in front of the class with her foot up on a stool. I could see right up the leg-hole of her shorts to her crutch-piece. This was my punishment for being a naughty boy.

My feelings towards girls began to change. They started to become not just nuisances who played silly games and messed up yours, but I began to 'see' something in girls that was worth exploring. My first girlfriend at school was Gillian Marchi. I remember fancying her, and the fact that her big brother was captain of Spurs made her even more attractive. I was a regular up the Spurs at the time. Everybody in the football world pronounced his name as Tony 'Mark-Eye'. I was better informed. It was Tony 'Markee'. 'No, it's not.' 'Oh yes it is, 'cos I go out with his sister.' Anything I said about football from then on was taken as gospel.

At school I was quite reasonable at football. I always wanted to be better, and I had a lot to live up to. My brother Dave played for Edmonton. I played in goal for the school and I thought I was pretty good but I never progressed from there. I really did want to be as good as him at football. I'll tell you something now that will make me sound like a rotten little sod when I was a kid. I buried all his football medals in the front garden. I must have been so fed up with relations coming round admiring 'em and saying 'Why ain't you got any?' I couldn't have been too bad though 'cos I owned up and dug 'em all up! Also, I did break the school record at the high jump. But shortly I was to have a go at music.

Playin' football, goin' up the Spurs, sport, fishing, even girls (for a while!) were about to take second place.

Chapter 5

I Become a Rock 'n' Roller

It was Little Richard that turned me onto Rock 'n' Roll. I was listening to Radio Luxembourg one night and he came on. I was gone! This was the most fantastic music I'd heard in my entire life! I went to school next day raving about him but nobody had heard of him. 'Just wait 'til you do. He sings a song called "Rip-it-up". He makes Bill Haley sound like Perry Como!' I wouldn't shut up about him. Not long after, me and my mates went to see 'The Girl Can't Help It'. Little Richard sang 'Ready Teddy' in the film. This was *real* Rock 'n' Roll. My mates had to own up, and I wanted to be in there *playing* Rock 'n' Roll.

I was about to find out that taking up music wasn't as easy as taking up fishing or football. But it was gonna be harder to put down.

I tried the piano but couldn't make head nor tail of it. Meanwhile other exciting Rock 'n' Rollers came along and the feeling of wanting to do what they were doing became an obsession. Fats Domino, Chuck Berry, Eddie Cochran and (although he wasn't Rock 'n' Roll but equally exciting in his own way) Lonnie Donegan. With him came skiffle groups. Washboards, tea-chest basses and guitars. *Guitar!* 'Now I think I'd get on alright with that,' I remember saying to my Mum who really did want there to be a musician in the family. 'Mum, I'd like to learn to play the guitar.' Mum promised she'd get hold of one for me if I promised to learn to play it. I did and she did.

It was an old Spanish guitar she got off my Uncle Alf. It was the same guitar she remembered having round the house when she was a kid. I went over to Uncle Alf's in Hackney to get it. I can still remember the smell of that guitar now. Uncle Alf had done it up. Filled all the cracks up with filler and given it a fresh coat of varnish. I arrived home proud. All I had to do now was to learn to play it and I was away. It looks pretty easy watchin' 'em play on the telly, I thought. I could strum alright so I was halfway there. It shouldn't take long.

'How long does it take to play a guitar?' It's a question I've often been asked. When they find the answer to 'How long is a piece of string?' perhaps I can answer it. If one bloke knows two chords and his mate knows none, his mate thinks the two-chorder can play the guitar. But he don't think so when he meets someone who knows four chords, and so on. In music you never stop learnin'. The advice I always give is to play every day, even if it is only five minutes every day. Now that don't sound long but you can bet your boots that once you've actually taken the step of pickin' up the guitar you won't put it down for at least an hour. Time flies when you are playing. Learn a new bit every day. Never think of the tenth step after the first, think of the second step. You'll reach the tenth step sooner than you know it (as long as you don't bang your head on the landing floor!)

I thought it was goin' to be easy but I pretty soon owned up that although my strummin' hand was reasonable, the noise that was comin' out was rough. It needs tuning up, I decided. But how do I do that? My Mum got close. She tuned it to a piano chord and I began to play it by stickin' one finger across frets at

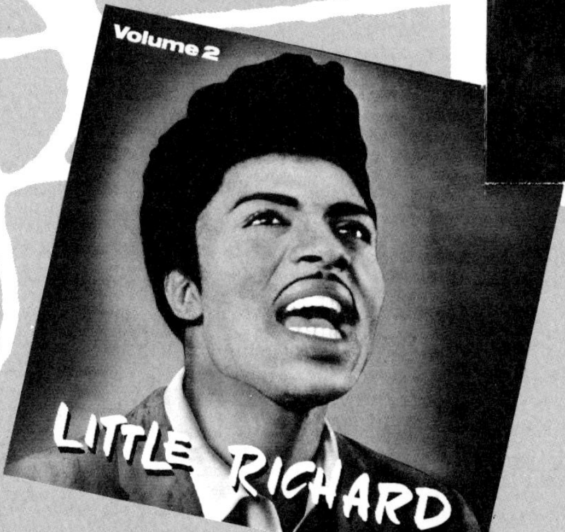

Uncle Alf (above left) gives me my first guitar and I set out to be like my heroes. Football and everything else takes a back seat.

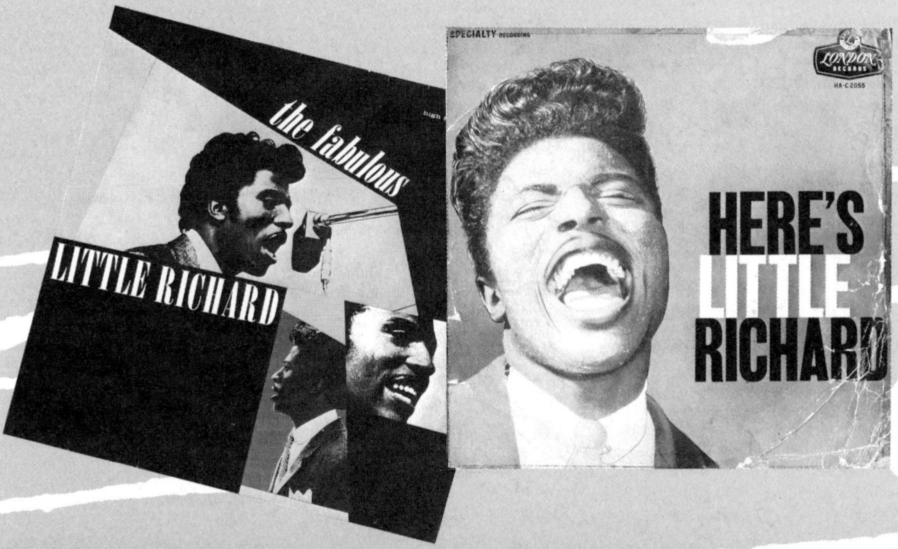
the fabulous
LITTLE RICHARD
SPECIALTY RECORDING
LONDON RECORDS
HERE'S LITTLE RICHARD

LITTLE RICHARD

different intervals to change to different chords. This didn't sound bad but I had a feeling it wasn't right. The guitar players I saw on the telly moved their fingers in different shapes. I had to find out why.

Skiffle goups were beginning to spring up all over the place and there was one down our street. Bob Weston over the road had one. There was talk about how good he was on the guitar. 'There's the man to tune your guitar,' Mum said. 'Catch him on his way home from work and ask him to tune it.' I waited at my front door one evening and waylaid him. He tuned it and impressed me with the few chords he casually strummed. I came runnin' in. I had found the key. Eureka! But when I ran my fingers over the strings it didn't sound as good as my Mum's tuning. (The proper guitar tuning is not tuned to a 'chord', so it doesn't sound very musical when played 'open', I found out later.) I was more confused than ever. I got hold of a chord book next, and things began to look a little clearer. When the right 'shapes' were played it began to sound reasonable.

My mum started me off. She figured out how to play the chords of 'Bring a Little Water, Sylvie'. She left off there, but I carried on. You made these notes on different parts of the fretboard. I now knew *how*. It was just a matter of time and practice. My next-door neighbour but one, Johnny Wright, played the banjo and he taught me a few chords. I began practising like mad and I began to get quite good on the guitar. Now, as it happened, Mum noticed an advert in the sweet shop window round the corner that said 'Guitarist/Banjo player wanted for the Horseshoe Skiffle Group'. That was Bob Weston's skiffle group, over the road. 'Go and have a go,' Mum said. I didn't think I was quite good enough yet, but she kept on and I did.

I not only passed the audition, but I knew I had really impressed 'em with my guitar and banjo playing. (I had bought an old banjo for a shilling at a jumble sale.) I was in the group! Mum was right. I must be better than I thought I was. The first paying gig I ever did ('Playing jobs' you called them in those days) was a hall over the top of the Britannia pub, Edmonton. Everyone remembers their first gig! We got paid as well! I felt a bit guilty about getting paid. It wasn't that we didn't play well. We played alright, but in my experience you got paid money for doing something you didn't like doin', not for something you loved doin' and would have done anyway. It didn't make sense. Nevertheless I got used to it.

The band got better and we did more and more gigs in and around North London. The personnel changed as the band progressed. An electric guitar was added and I wanted to put Rock 'n' Roll songs into the act. Little Richard's 'Rip-it-up' was the first and it didn't sound bad. Skiffle had been a big help to me, but I was ready to move on. Now I was a Rock 'n' Roller!

Chapter 6

Jerry Lee for Me

Skiffle had played its part, and an important part. It got me started. Throughout pop history a relatively simple type of music every now and then becomes popular. It is good because it makes kids think, 'Perhaps I can do that,' and they do, and in a short time some of them are sounding as good as the records. The serious ones move on from there, but that start is important.

Skiffle was like that. It progressed to Rock 'n' Roll and Blues (in England) and players like Eric Clapton and Albert Lee, whose roots lie in Skiffle, began to be popular. But not many kids, in their wildest dreams, thought they could pick up a guitar and learn something quick that sounded like them. They were too far advanced. Something simpler was needed to give the kids the feeling again of 'I can do that!' Then Bob Dylan came round and thousands of youngsters overnight bought guitars and were strummin' 'Blowin' in the Wind' in parks, on Tube trains, in the streets, everywhere, and most of 'em sounded as good as him. 'New Wave Skiffle!' The next time it happened was Punk. These were really important eras for getting new musicians off the ground. But back to the Horseshoe Skiffle Group.

We were now a Rock 'n' Roll group. We were called The Horseshoes and did songs like 'Ready Teddy', 'That'll Be the Day', 'Oh Boy!', 'Let's Have a Party' – the choice of material was limitless. Up till now I'd experienced all my Rock 'n' Roll idols on film or on record. I'd never seen any of 'em live. I'd missed the Buddy Holly concerts at the Regal, Edmonton. I don't know why I didn't go, I can't remember. All the kids at school went and were ravin' about him. P'raps that's what made me determined not to miss the next concert at the Regal. It was to be Jerry Lee Lewis.

That performance was a milestone in my life. The line-up was piano, bass and drums (coincidence: that is me and Dave's line-up now; or is it coincidence?). They had an electric bass, the first I'd ever seen, the loudest drummer I'd ever heard, and Jerry Lee playin' piano like it was a new instrument. I had a piano indoors, but it never sounded like that! I still loved Little Richard, but this man played music that was even closer to my heart. His piano playing, although I hadn't heard anything like it before, made sense. This was the way I'd like to play piano if I ever became a pianist.

I liked the songs he sang and the way he sang 'em. I decided then and there I'd catch as many of his English tour gigs as possible before he went home. Two days later he was deported. All because he married some 13-year-old girl! I couldn't believe it! The Home Office decided he would be a bad influence on us youngsters. 'Are they mad? Don't they realise that me and the rest just like him for his music. They're protecting us?' I was beside myself with rage. What he did in his private life didn't concern me in the least. Of course I was right but the letter I wrote to the Home Office didn't make any difference. They kicked him out and that was that. If someone had've told me then that one day I'd record an album with him, sing a duet and do gigs with him, and he'd record a song I helped write, what would I have said? 'You're mad!' But he did!

That Jerry Lee concert was in May 1958 and at that time I was coming up to school-leaving age. I'd had fun at school despite the ups and downs. I learnt to play guitar while I was at school and my first attempt at Skiffle was also at school. Me and Brian Juniper used to have a few sessions round his house. (It was through Brian that I met Dave Peacock much later. Brian was in the same junior school as Dave and formed a group with Dave when he left school.) My headmaster now and again threw a few compliments my way. I couldn't handle that. It was out of character. He'd come into the class and give a lecture on the evils of hanging around street corners late at night. 'Why not take a leaf out of Hodges' book and learn to play a musical instrument?' I almost thought, 'He's not so bad after all.' The music teacher never gave me any encouragement, though. All Rock 'n' Roll was rubbish in his book. I marked him down as a know-nuffink.

But my being in favour with the Headmaster was short-lived. It was Christmas 1958 and the School Party.

It was the year canned beer was introduced and it was a bit of a novelty. Me and my mates decided to have a go and bought some Long Life to drink in the school bog. We had a line of cans set up along the top of the toilet doors. Me and my mate Don Philips were just drainin' the last dregs out of our cans ready to go back and join the party. I said (feelin' really big), 'I bet ol' Dunnie (the Head) would do his bollocks if he walked in now!'

I sensed a presence as I said it. I lowered my eyeballs as I was guzzling, and they fell upon a pair of horribly familiar baggy trousers. In 'em stood the

The Regal as it was until they pulled it down a few years ago.

Aged 14. The barnet becomes important!

Above Jerry Lee at the Regal, Edmonton in 1958. I believe this picture was taken backstage. The suit was bright red, the hair was yellow. The man played the piano like I'd never seen before. I was hooked.

Jerry Lee Lewis
LONDON
A SUN RECORDING

headmaster. Without a word he took the empty beer cans from us and once more it was 'lookin' thru' the legs time'.

The next morning we were both hauled up in front of the school and were asked to leave at the Christmas holidays. I was actually 14 when I left (or was politely expelled) but I was 15 just after Christmas, so legally able to start work, which I did.

Chapter 7
First Real Job

The first job I got was at Turners, the jeweller's shop on Edmonton Green, as a watch and clockmaker's apprentice. My Mum knew the Governor, who used to go in the Exhibition pub where she played piano. My brother worked there when he left school a couple of years earlier, but he didn't get on with the job and moved on.

The idea of messing about with old clocks, takin' 'em apart and puttin' 'em back together appealed to me. I asked Mum if she could get me a job there. I went up to be interviewed and I started in January 1959. I liked that job. At the time I had never dreamed of earnin' a livin' playin' music. I never knew anyone who was a professional musician. I had a job and as far as 'proper' jobs go, it wasn't bad. It was a little old 19th-century shop. I was on my own most of the time. I became quite good at mendin' old clocks quite quickly, though I wasn't mad on watchmending. All you did with watches was find out what was wrong and send away for a new part. But clocks; some of the old ones you'd get in, you'd have to use your initiative, and make new parts to get them going. The feelin' of bringin' them old clocks back to life was a nice feelin'.

I worked hard when I was there but I was constantly late for work. I couldn't get up in the mornings, and I still can't. I hated mornings and still do. I'm a different person in the morning and always have been. Regardless of what time I go to bed. I'm not proud of the fact, I'm just being honest about myself. It's nothing to do with hangovers or anything like that. I was the same when I was at school. I am not very well tempered in the mornings and don't want to speak to anybody. I get annoyed at stupid things that I'm ashamed of later in the day. When me and me brother had to get up together to go to school, we wouldn't speak. But the sound of him crunching his toast used to make me want to punch him! Now ain't that terrible?

I become a different person after midday and when I think of my instinctive feelings earlier that morning I am ashamed. I mean, 'Stop crunchin' that fuckin' toast!' WALLOP! What a little bastard! Thank Christ it wears off. I make a point of avoiding mornings at all costs, though sometimes I can't. I feel I'm being victimised when I'm woke up in the morning to go and do something. I do it – but grudgingly. And them bright and breezy morning people! I feel they're bein' like they are just to annoy me. It can't be natural. It can't be natural to be laughin' and jokin' while it's still mornin'. They're doin' it just 'cos they know it annoys me! Once again in the afternoon I'm thoroughly ashamed of myself. I'm thinkin', I really had the hump with him this morning, laughin' and jokin' like that. I can tolerate him now and he's still laughin' and jokin'. But now it's afternoon.

The best thing I've learned to do in the morning is to keep my mouth shut and don't say nothing. As I said, I'm not proud of it and if the two of me ever met, the morning me and the afternoon or evening me, well, I don't think they'd get on too well together. The evening me would not tolerate such a short-tempered little git as the morning me, and the morning me would not tolerate such a cheerful genial chap as the evening me.

When I started that job at Turners, the Governor was off sick and his son Charley took over 'til he became well. Charley was a good bloke. He'd moan at me for being late but he knew I worked well when I did get in so it never got to the sack. But when the Governor got back he couldn't accept my tardiness and I was soon given an ultimatum: 'Get in early or get out.' I couldn't see the sense. All the work got done on time even if I had to take work home to finish it. I didn't mind, I enjoyed it. But I didn't like mornings and I couldn't get up in time. I turned up late again to be greeted by the Governor with me cards. 'Oh fuck him,' I thought, 'if he can't see I'm a good worker then bollocks.' I was earning more money playing local gigs than I was working there anyway.

The Horseshoes by this time had drifted apart and I began playing with new musicians. I met up with Tony Ollard, a great guitar player. We began swapping ideas. We started playin' gigs at the King's Head, Edmonton – a good Rock 'n' Roll gig. The King's Head was a great meeting place (I also met my wife there!). There really were some good musicians in and around North London at that time and the King's Head was a good place to find 'em on a Friday night. For a while I was in no regular band. Whoever was available just got together and away we went. Invaluable experience. The musicians got to know each other, swapped ideas, talked about guitars and Rock 'n' Roll. I had found a crowd I could identify with. The bass guitar began to be talked about. Not many had seen one, let alone heard one, apart from on Rock 'n' Roll records. I had seen one. Jerry Lee's bass player had one. I fancied playin' bass. I fancied playin' double bass at one time, but it wasn't practical. It wouldn't fit in the luggage compartment on the bus like the old tea chest used to! On some Friday night gigs, four or five guitar players would turn up. We made a bit of a row sometimes. We were still young and our tunin' quite often was not spot on. One night I tuned my bass strings down a couple of tones and played sort of bass lines. Were the boys impressed!! So was I. A new sound! I had discovered a frequency range uncluttered by anybody else's, and it sounded good. That was it, I was going to become an electric bass player. I saw an advert for a Hofner Bass Guitar that you could buy on the knock from Bell Accordions in Surbiton, Surrey. My Grandad signed as guarantor, the deposit was sent off and the guitar arrived.

I tried it out indoors in my little amp, playing along to records. It sounded absolutely fantastic! I couldn't wait to get together with the boys at the King's Head. Up Town Road I went early on Friday evening, amp in one hand, bass guitar in the other. I arrived, proud, at the gig.

As I was plugging in my amp, the rest of the boys were admiring my guitar. 'Blimey, ain't the strings thick. It's fantastic.' 'You wait 'til you hear it,' I said. I tuned it up sittin' close to me amp and away we went. Did that bass sound good? It sounded fuckin' terrible! 'Fart, Rasp, Rattle.' I couldn't beleive it. In my front room it sounded great but my poor little amp couldn't cope with the rest of the band in that big hall. I never knew that a bass needed a bigger speaker and cabinets, etc.

'I don't think you realise what you let yourself in for, Chas,' said Billy Kuy, the guitar player. 'You're gonna have to fork out for a bigger amp and you won't be able to carry it up and down Town Road like you can that one.' I didn't want to believe him but I knew he was right. It was an obstacle that had to be

Above The King's Head, Edmonton, where I learned my rock 'n' roll and met my wife Joan. **Left** Mike Berry, me and the famous bass amp that belonged to The Shadows, which I gave to Dave and he sawed up. I've still got the hump about it.

overcome. I was hooked on the bass guitar.

Now although I didn't have a bass amp, I suddenly found myself in demand by all the bands that played down the King's Head. Bands were willing to provide a bass amp if I would sit in with 'em. No-one else in Edmonton had a bass guitar. It made their band sound professional and I weren't complaining. I was earning money playing with all these bands. Playing the bass gave me the chance to work with nearly all the musicians around North London and eventually a band was formed which I was pleased to become a part of: Billy Gray and The Stormers. Me on bass, Reg Hawkins rhythm guitar, Billy Kuy lead guitar, Billy (Gray) Halsey singer, and Bobby Neate on drums. This was the band for me and I thought it was time I got a bass amp of my own. Bobby Neate had an open-backed van. He had to carry his drums but there was enough room for a proper bass amp. He agreed to lug it about if I got one. So I set to work.

Billy Kuy told me that the bass player with Dave Sampson and the Hunters, Johnny Rogers, had a bass amp for sale. He'd bought it from Jet Harris, the Shadows' bass player. I'd seen Cliff and the Shadows when Jet Harris was using the amp. I thought it was fantastic. Johnny Rogers wanted £20 for the lot. I was round there like a shot and got it.

Now this bass amp was built like a little house and was about as heavy as one. It was about 4 foot high, 3 foot wide and 3 foot deep. A solid wooden box (2 inch thick wood) within a box and the cavity was filled with sand. You can imagine the weight. It was made by Wallace in Soho Street. I think it was the first British bass amp ever made. Bobby Neate, who had promised to lug it about, looked a bit dismayed when he found out what he'd agreed to. But he didn't back out and it came with us on the road. It had a sound and half! (Some years later I gave that cabinet to some geezer I'd just met named Dave Peacock. He sawed a fuckin' great hole in it, all the sand fell out and it ended up in his back garden. It's probably still there now!)

Billy Gray and The Stormers began to get a name as the best band round North London. Through someone or other we heard that there were auditions going for Butlins Holiday Camps. We brushed up the act and went for the audition at the Majestic in Finsbury Park. There were some good bands there from all over London. We had competition. But a few days later we got a letter through saying that we had passed. We were to go to Filey Holiday Camp in Yorkshire for the 1960 summer season at £20 each a week. An absolute fortune for a 16 year-old and all we had to do was play music! I couldn't wait to get there and it was to turn out even better than I had expected.

Chapter 8
Butlins with Billy Gray and The Stormers

It was heaven. Parties every night, go to bed when you like, get up when you like, a new girlfriend every week. You'd watch 'em file in to the dance on the night of arrival, smile at the one you fancied and you were away! I never knew it was as easy pulling birds. Why didn't I try this before? I wasn't used to all this!

I'd had a couple of girlfriends in the past. I was courting a girl who I packed up just before I went to Butlins. I shan't ever forget that. I was courting her for about three months. At the time I thought I was in love. We'd have rows and at the end she'd say, 'Go on then, *go* if you want to.' And me like a fool didn't, and would talk her round. I remember thinking if ever I wanted to pack her up it would be easy, she wouldn't give a monkeys. One mornin' I woke up and I remember thinkin', I don't want to see her anymore. There was no feeling or nothing. The worm had turned. So, I didn't go round her house. It was easy. After a week I'd forgotten all about her. Then there came a knock on the door. I looked out of the window and it was her with her mate. I was getting ready to go up the King's Head at the time.

'Hello,' I said. 'What do you want?'

'I want my Ricky Nelson records!' she said.

'Oh alright, I'll chuck 'em out of the window to you.'

'No, bring 'em down. I want to talk to you. Anyway, I might miss 'em and they might break.'

I didn't want to talk to her. It was all finished as far as I was concerned. I didn't want to break her records, though. I went downstairs. They were only 45s, I'll probably be able to poke 'em through the letterbox. But they were just too big. I opened the door quick, stuck 'em in her hand and went to shut the door, but she was there pushing on the door from the other side with all her might to keep it open. I managed to shut the door, then:

'Whaaaaaaaa!' she started cryin'. She just sort of switched it on. It frightened me.

'Shut up!' I shouted through the letter-box.

'Whaaaaa!' she said.

'Shut up and I'll come out!' I shouted again. I thought the whole street must be out. She stopped. I opened the door.

'I want you to come back to me. Whaaaaa!'

'Shut up!' I said.

'What's the matter?' shouted Nan from the front room.

'Nothing, Nan.' I went out to the doorstep and shut the door.

'I think we should finish with each other,' I said.

Butlin's Days. **Top** Bobbie Graham, Billy Kuy, Reg Hawkins, Billy Gray and me. **Above right** Grant, the camp barber (I mean 'camp' as in holiday camp, I think – oh, never mind!), Billy Kuy and me. **Above left** Reg, girl, me, bloke, girl and Billy Gray.

'Whaaaaaa!'

Oh, bleedin' hell, the street'll think she's bein' murdered.

'Just let me come with you to the King's Head tonight.'

'No!'

'Whaaaa!'

'Alright, just be quiet. I'll walk you to the bus stop but you can't come *in* to the King's Head.'

Silence. What a relief! 'Alright,' she said.

'Let me get me coat and me bass.' I was in and out like a shot and off we went up the street. All the time she kept askin' 'Why?' I didn't know why, I just knew I'd got fed up with her. On top of that the more she pleaded the more I didn't want to know. At the top of the road I suddenly decided to leave her there.

'I'm goin' and you're not comin' with me.'

'Whaaaaa!'

'Alright, stop it, I'll walk on a bit further.'

Silence. 'What am I goin' to do?' I asked myself. 'This is goin' to go on forever.' I finally made the decision as we were taking a short cut through the alley to the bus stop.

'I'm goin'', I said, and I went.

'Whaaaaaaaaaaa!'

I couldn't have left her in a worse place. The echo between those two brick walls in that alley was deafening. This girl who once could twist me round her little finger, hollering like that! I was confused but I felt I was doing the right thing. Anyway, soon I'd be off to Butlins and having the time of my life.

I lived for the moment and Butlins was the moment. But it was going to end only too quick.

At the end of the summer we came back home and I thought, 'Oh well, it's a shame that's over but we're bound to get loads of gigs, so it won't be so bad.' But two of the band got married and the interest waned. So did the gigs. I had to get a job.

Down the employment exchange I've gone with Billy Kuy. I was asked all the usual questions.

'What did you like at school?'

'Nothin'. Well, football and woodwork.'

'Right, I can't fix you up with a job at the Spurs, but there's a job goin' at a woodwork factory in Edmonton. Get down there.'

Off I've gone.

Now Billy Kuy had always worked in office jobs. He wore detachable collars and you never ever saw him without a tie. There were no office jobs going at the factory, but he was skint. He was no good at woodwork but the man at the employment exchange said they needed someone sweepin' up, so Bill came too. On the way I've thought, 'Oh well, makin' somethin' out of wood might not be so bad.' I remembered making a split-cane fishin' rod and a veneered cigarette box at school and I quite enjoyed it. We've turned up at the factory, Billy Kuy has been given a broom and off he's gone.

'Right, Mr. Hodges, come over here.' It was a deck-chair makin' factory. Not very creative, but makin' the best of it I am thinkin' p'raps I can get into it.

Drillin' the holes, shapin' the wood, fittin' the canvas, sanding down and polishing and being proud of the finished product. Yeh, it won't be so bad.

'Right, Mr Hodges, here's what you do. See them sticks with holes in?'

'Yeh.'

'Well, put them round sticks in them round holes and bang a nail in to stop 'em comin' out.'

'Right. What do I do next?'

'That lot over there,' he said, pointing to a mountain of sticks with holes in and hole-shaped sticks.

'If you need any more nails, come and see me.'

I've never seen a bigger tin of nails! It was like a bad dream. There was I, left all alone with a pile of sticks that had to be banged together. A monkey would have been humiliated at the task. I made a start. In front of me was a dingy window that hadn't been cleaned for years. Through it I could see a blurred vision of the bright autumn sunshine. I'm thinkin', 'This time last week I was at Butlins Holiday Camp. Heaven and Hell! Yes, that's it, I'm in Hell. This is what it must be like.'

I've managed to get through to tea-break, then I saw Billy Kuy. That depressed me even more. The Jack the Lad of the band, number one bird puller, smooth talker, always wore a clean collar, man about town, looked a wreck. There he was, no collar, hair all over the place, red face, sweepin' up. He's come over to me with his broom.

'Chas, I've had enough, I am fuckin' off home!'

'Go, Bill,' I said. As much as he got on me nerves sometimes, with his smoothie ways and dapper habits back at Butlins, I didn't want to see him like this. 'Go, Bill,' I said. 'I'm gonna stick it out, I think.'

Bill's gone. Dinner-time come and I'm fed up and depressed and everything. I've gone out to get me bike to go home for dinner. I can't find me bike. Some bastard's pinched me bike! Right, that's it. I've had enough. How can I work with a load of thievin' bastards! I'm not havin' it. That's the last time I'm comin' to work here.

On the way home I began to feel happier. Although me bike was pinched it gave me the excuse to leave. 'I mean, you can't expect me to work with a bunch of thieves,' I've told me Mum when I've got home. 'I mean, what are they gonna pinch next?'

'Well, you've got to earn some money somewhere, Chas,' said Mum. 'So you'd better start thinkin'.' My usually easy-going Mum was right and I knew it. I've gone back on Friday to get me cards and me morning's money and I'm just goin' out of the gate when someone said:

'Oi, you, come here. Did you come here on a yellow bike?'

'Yes,' I said, 'and one of your mob's nicked it!'

'Nicked it? We brought it in out of the rain. It's in the shed over there.'

I felt rotten the way I'd run 'em down. I called 'em all the bastards under the sun and all they'd done was bring it in for me 'cos it was gettin' wet in the rain. They weren't so bad after all. But the thought of going back to that job filled me with dread. I couldn't wait to get away from the place. But I was out of work and the band by now had split. What do I do next?

Chapter 9
The Outlaws

Just before The Stormers split we did a couple of test recordings and also backed a singer called Danny Rivers who we met at Butlins on a couple of demos. Danny Rivers had a couple of brief spots on 'Oh Boy'. He sung 'Stuck on You' on one appearance, but had trouble reaching the high note in the middle.

'Tear' was the word. The line was, 'A team of wild horses couldn't "tear" (high note) us apart.' Jack Good got Dickie Pride to sing 'tear' behind the scene while Danny mimed the word. It worked. You'd never have spotted it if you didn't know.

Danny was managed by Peter Yaquinandi who was a bit of a character. One night not many days after the bike pinchin' episode fate took a hand. There was a knock on my door. It was Peter Yaquinandi, or 'Yak' as we called him. He was managing a singer called Mike Berry who had passed an audition with an independent recording engineer named Joe Meek. Joe was well impressed with Mike Berry but not too impressed with his band. Yak was on his way round to see the rest of our band. If he could get them back together, would I be willing to audition at Joe Meek's as a backing musician to Mike Berry? He played me some demo tapes and Mike was like Buddy Holly (not like but almost *him*!). Buddy Holly ranked highly among my Rock heroes along with Jerry Lee Lewis and Little Richard.

I was all for it. The rest of the boys agreed: Reg Hawkins on rhythm guitar, Billy Kuy on lead (ex-broom!) and Bobby Neate (who now called himself Bobby Graham) on drums. An audition with Joe Meek was arranged. We passed the audition and before we knew it we had a record out on the market. My first record! 'Will You Love Me Tomorrow' by Mike Berry and The Outlaws (Joe's new name for us). That one didn't do too good, but soon after The Outlaws recorded 'Swingin' Low' which made the Top 50. We were on our way, but the chart thing was really an extra for me. The main thing was, I was back playing and enjoying myself. The deck-chair factory? A bad dream I'd woken up from!

Joe Meek was alright. By that I mean that his heart was in the right place. He was a bit of a bum boy, as I found out later. At the time I met him, though, I'd heard these stories about blokes stickin' their winkles up other blokes' bums – but who could really believe that? I mean, I was told havin' a Jodrell sent ya blind and – and, well, I could go on for ever! I was 16 years of age. Old enough to realise that schoolboys told these fairy tales to each other while havin' a crafty dog end round the back of the bike sheds. But I was in for a shock.

A mate of mine, Tony Ollard, played me a tape he'd got from somewhere, of some guitar playing. I'd never heard the like of it before. He told me he thought it was a bloke called Chet Atkins but he didn't know who the other bloke was. I thought it could be one bloke double-tracked. Later on I found out it *was* Chet Atkins but it wasn't double-tracked. The man just played like two guitar players! I begged Tony to lend me the tape and I'd get it copied and return it straight away. Who do I know who's got two tape recorders? Joe Meek! Next time we did a session I asked Joe if he'd do a copy of this tape for me.

'Bring it up tomorrow and I'll do it.' I was there. He's done the tape, I was well pleased, caught the last bus home and played that tape till the sun came up. Next day I'm ravin' about this tape to the boys.

'Never mind the tape', they said. 'What about Joe? Did he give you one?'

'Bollocks!' I've gone, 'he's alright, how old are you?' Christ, some people just don't grow up, do they?

Now Joe wrote most of the instrumentals for the band. I say 'wrote', his method was more like 'get an idea for a tune, find a record that was the right tempo and sing his tune to it'. The resulting demo (which I had to decipher) was a din; he sang out of tune too. I had to work out what I *thought* he was trying to get across. Most of it I figured out but I had to put my own bits in for the bits I couldn't decipher. Joe always seemed pleased with the result, so all was well. Anyway he'd invite me up to listen to his latest creation and I'd take the acetate home and try to make it playable by the band.

This happened on many occasions. Not a move was made, bum-boy-wise. Ol' Joe's alright!

One Saturday afternoon I've gone up there to listen to another Joe Meek 'composition', heard it, worked it out with difficulty, and worked out how we're gonna do it. Got it! Great! Ready to go home.

'Do you want a cup of coffee 'fore you go, Chas?'

'Alright, Joe.' I can remember feeling a bit uneasy, but 'He's alright', I told myself. In his sitting room he had this sofa. No matter where you sat on it, you were sort of bounced towards the middle and ended up sittin' next to whoever else was on it. Even if you both sat down at the extreme ends of the sofa, which we did. There we was, me and Joe. 'I hope my mates are wrong,' I'm thinking as we sat together in the middle of the sofa. Now in them days wrestling was just becoming popular, and Joe had it on the telly. It was popular in the Sixties and was always on of a Saturday afternoon. As I'm trying to knock back the cup of coffee he made me which had too much sugar in it – funny how you remember silly details – Joe said to me:

'I love wrestling, do you?'

My whole life flashed before me. I thought, 'Oh no! It's the *bums* he likes! My mates were right.' Too late! The next minute, there was a hand groping round my bollocks and I froze. Petrified. It must have been only a fraction of a second that I sat there rigid but it was enough to make Joe think, 'He likes it.' 'Cos his hand started scrunching quicker and he started bobbing up and down. My eyes started watering. I looked at Joe. His eyeballs were bulging but he looked ever so happy. I leapt out of that seat like my arsehole was alight! (It would have been if I'd stayed much longer!) I found my voice but the best I could come out with was:

'I've got to be going now. I've got to go and meet my big brother.' I had always mentioned my 'big' brother when I was threatened by anybody at school. It was the best I could think of. I was out of his flat like a shot. I kept running until I saw a bus that was heading in the general direction of home and I leapt on it. The conductor asked for me fare in a normal voice and I felt safe. I was back in the land of the un-bum boys.

Next day, though, I thought, 'I believe now there *are* blokes that stick their winkles up other blokes' bums.' I was growing up. I rang Mike Berry and told him of the episode.

'The dirty bastard,' was all he kept saying between the gaps in my story.

'Yes,' I said in the end. 'Isn't he?' I never spoke to Joe for days afterwards but as I started to weigh it up I thought, 'Well, it does go on; but at least I got away and didn't get raped.' I s'pose it's the same as some geezer fancyin' some bird. He weren't to know I liked birds and not geezers. He fancied me so he had to find out. But now he's found out he knows where he stands. He rung up and apologised a couple of days later. 'That's OK, Joe,' I said, 'but let's have no more of it.' That was the end of that, but Charlie Hodges could now say, when the subject of bum boys came up: 'Oh yes, it goes on alright. You don't believe it? Oh, come now. How naive can you get!'

Joe with all his eccentricities was well before his time in the recording field. DI-ing the bass, for instance, was a matter of course for Joe. DI-ing or Direct Injection (nothing to do with bum boys!) meant the bass player didn't use an amp. The bass was plugged more or less direct into the tape machine. No amp was used in the actual studio and this meant there were no stray notes or 'booms' floatin' around to be picked up by other microphones. This technique meant a much cleaner and purer sound for the electric bass. All studios do it now. Joe always had five or six mikes on the drum kit instead of one or two which was usual for the time. He loved a sound that had 'presence'. He wanted to hear the snare drum, hi-hat, bass drum, cymbals *close*. It worked. They all do this now. Joe would have been in his element with a multi-track machine. He never got one as far as I know; they were still a novelty in England when Joe died not many years later.

Now The Outlaws were doing alright. We were out on the road with Mike Berry and started doing a few sessions up at Joe Meek's. Joe was always recording somebody or the other. Most of 'em never came to anything but we did some sessions with an actor, John Leyton. 'Johnny Remember Me' was one of the songs we did, and suddenly *I* was on a Number One Hit. My friends and relations thought I was rich, but you got £7. 10s a session regardless of whether it was a hit or not. I earned far more off Joe's flops. I thought this fair enough, still do, but they'd go, 'What! *He* got all that money and all *you* got was £7. 10s?' They probably thought I'd copped a fortune, and was keeping it dark.

We did a few other recordings with John Leyton. Amongst 'em was the follow-up, 'Wild Wind', on which I played fretless bass. It had frets on it at the beginning of the session, but I got this idea halfway through that a bass guitar without frets might sound a bit like a double bass. I couldn't wait to try it so levered 'em out on the session. It didn't sound too bad. As far as I knew it was *the* first fretless bass guitar. But it didn't last long. I kept pitchin' the notes all wrong on harder sessions, so I put the frets back.

We backed John Leyton for a week in Brighton later on. There was a bit in 'Wild Wind' he used to sing which I thought was comical. He sung the song in an American accent but when he got to the word 'trouble' he sort of went all cockney. It was the best part of the whole song for me but I'm not sure he meant it to be a laugh. You see, he had to really holler that word to get it out as it was the highest note in the whole song. He had to really open his mouth wide. Now you can't sing 'trouble' in American style ('trerble') with your mouth wide open like a barrow boy's. It *has* to come out as 'trubball'. Good though.

That original Outlaws band was a good line-up. Bill, Bob, Reg and me. Reg was a *real* rhythm guitarist. Not like most of them. In those days most of them were frustrated lead guitarists. He was my best mate in the band, and we still see a lot of each other today. Dave likes Reg, too. He's got a great sense of humour and is always good company. I first met Reg at Higher Grade School. He was a year older than me but him and his mate, and me and my mate, Rodney Clark, used to knock around together. It was unusual to mix with anyone in a different year to you but we all used to laugh at the same things.

It was coincidence that we ended up in the same band together. We lost touch after we left school then met again a few years later up the King's Head (the birthplace of The Outlaws).

I was with Reg when I learnt my first chords on the piano. Apart from having the same taste in humour we also had the same taste in music. He introduced me to the music of Jack Elliot and Derrol Adams. We both loved Big Bill Broonzy and Chet Atkins. We'd sit around for hours on end doing our best to copy 'em. We were both Jerry Lee fans too. When we were at Butlins we found out there was a way of sneaking into the Viennese Ball Room after it was shut. It had a grand piano! We'd sit up all night singing and I began to get off some bits I thought sounded like Jerry Lee. How much like Jerry Lee it was I

Early Outlaw days. **Top** Mike Berry and me on the Firth of Forth ferry. Scottish tour, 1961. **Above** Me and Reg in Brighton, relaxing during a hard week backing John Leyton.

don't know, but Reg liked it and that gave me encouragement.

Bobbie Graham was a great drummer. A bit of a jazzer when he joined us, I don't think he was too mad on Rock 'n' Roll and I don't think he was too mad on me at the time, trying to get him to play like Jerry Lee's drummer. Perhaps I was too young to explain what I meant. I knew Bob was a better *drummer* than Jerry Lee's but the *feel* wasn't right. (I don't even think the musical term 'feel' was used in those days, I just used to say, 'It don't sound *right*, Bob'.) He did eventually get into Rock 'n' Roll (p'raps I wore him down) and there was no one to touch him.

Billy Kuy? Now what can I say about ol' Bill? A bit short-tempered in his younger days (to say the least!) but you could have a laugh with him. He knew his instrument and was particularly good at chords.

I remember saving Bill's life once. Me and Bill had just finished a gig at The Angel, Edmonton. Irish John, my stepfather, told me there was a party going after hours over the top of the 'Ex'. I asked Bill if he fancied going, his eyes lit up and off we went.

We had to walk through Edmonton Green on the way. Now Edmonton Green was renowned for pulling bits of stray after dark and Bill spotted a bit of stray. But the bit he spotted (Bill wasn't to know and probably wouldn't have

Three records in the Top 30 in 1961 and still skint – but happy! 'Wild Wind' (2), 'Johnny Remember Me' (17) and 'Tribute to Buddy Holly' (24).

cared anyway as he was three-parts pissed) was the dodgiest bit of stray in Edmonton. Everyone knew her (except Bill).

Bill's homed in and started giving her the 'Billy Kuy chat'. 'Bill, you're mad,' I tell him. 'Come here.'

Too late. He's back with her on his arm and a big 'Look what I got' smile on his face. He's invited her to the party.

Anyway we've arrived, seen Irish John, we're in. Straight up to the bar. Great. I'd forgotten about the bird, so had Bill. It was me and Bill, after-hours in a pub.

'What d'yer want to drink, Chas?'

'I'll have a pint, Bill.' I've gone off to the bog.

I've come back. No Bill. *Now* where's he gone? He's supposed to be getting the pints in.

I've looked round, and there he is. Rabbitin' away nineteen to the dozen to some great big Irishman. The look on Bill's face told me it wasn't no matey conversation. Bill was wild-eyed, and by the look on the Irishman's face he was none too friendly either.

I've gone to the rescue. As I've got near, I've recognised the Irishman, Big Mick, one of my stepfather's workmates. Bill's picked on a wrong 'un this time! I've moved in.

'Hallo Mick,' I've gone. 'How ya doin'?' He's looked round, wild an' all, but soon as he saw me he softened a little.

'Chassy boy! How yer fluten doin'?' Thank God he's recognised me. I've breathed (for Bill's sake) a sigh of relief.

'Not too bad, Mick. What d'ya want t'drink?'

'Oh, I'll have a wee Scotch with ya, Chassy boy.'

I've done it! I thought. But no.

'Oh no you fuckin' won't!' says Bill. Mick's friendly look changed back to the wild one again.

'You little git! Oi'l morder ye!' he's said, leaping at Bill's throat.

'Hold up, hold up, hold up!' I've gone. 'Look, Mick! Talk to *me!* What's the matter?'

I've moved round the front so he can see my eyes. He's dropped Bill.

'He says I've been chatting up his girlfriend. Oi wasn't! I swear oi was only *talking* to the woman!'

I believed Mick, but I couldn't believe Bill. Getting all possessive over this 'ol bird! He'd forgotten all about her a minute ago. I've given him a look, as if to say, 'Are you mad? This bloke's three times the size of you! Bugger off quick while you're in one piece.'

'Look, Mick,' I've said, 'me and Bill's been out and had a few pints. We're both a bit pissed. Let's forget it, come on I'll buy you that Scotch.'

Mick would've gone for it, but oh no.

'*I'm* not pissed, Chas.' 'Oh, *shutup,* Bill!' 'And your Irish mate's a cunt!'

With that Mick's gone for Bill in a big way, and he *meant* it. He's lifted Bill up like a bit of rag and pushed him through the nearest door. Which happened to be the bog-hole. I've run in, and there was Mick with Bill on the floor, trying to grind his head in the piss trough with his boot. Bill's head was jerking from left to right, deftly dodging every stomp, but it would have been only a matter of time.

'Mick!' I've hollered, grabbing hold of him. Mick's turned round ready to take a swing, then saw it was me.

'Mick,' I said. 'Leave him alone. He's not worth the bother. Come and have a drink.'

Mick was torn between two emotions. Bill at last saw the light and was up and away. I dragged Mick to the bar and bought him that Scotch.

Bill did end up fighting someone that night. It was Freddy the Fly, a mate of ours. They had a punch-up all up and down Edmonton Market. I don't know why, but it was the way Bill liked to round his evenings off.

Around 1962 the original Outlaws folded up. Reg decided the business wasn't for him and settled down with a regular job. Bob joined Joe Brown and Bill buggered off somewhere or other. That left me and Mike Berry.

If I remember right, the first new Outlaw was drummer Don Groom. In fact I think he did a couple of gigs with Reg and Bill before they left. Mike got hold of Ray 'Biffo' Byhart to play rhythm guitar, so now we had drums, rhythm and bass. All we needed was a lead guitarist.

Mike heard about this lead guitarist who had been working with Screaming Lord Sutch (Sutch had a reputation for finding good Rock 'n' Rollers). But the guitarist would only consider joining if we took his piano-playing mate on too. We didn't want a piano player, but we thought we'd get 'em down and if we liked the guitarist we'd talk him into joining us on his own.

They've both turned up, and I've never seen such a weird-looking couple of geezers. The guitar player was about 4 foot 6 tall with bleached blonde hair and a face straight out of a Brueghel painting. The piano player was about 6 foot tall, as skinny as a rake and looked dopey. Neither one of 'em hardly said a word. 'Oh, well,' I've thought. 'Let's get it over and done with, think of something diplomatic to say as to why we don't want 'em, and think again.'

Now I want you to try to imagine how a young, enthusiastic and talented Rock 'n' Roller looked at things in those days. You see, we knew the *feel* of our music, but we weren't particularly *masters* of our instruments. We simply hadn't been playing long enough to become so and any player that was nimble or 'fast', as we called it, gained our immediate admiration. But usually the ones that were fast didn't have the feel and vice versa.

Anyway, I'm plugging in me bass, thinking about who can we ring tomorrow who might know of a lead guitarist, when I heard a sound that made me freeze. It really did. My life for two seconds was in suspended animation. I can remember how far the jack plug was from the hole and everything.

'DIDDLY DIDDLY DIDDLY DIDDLY DUM BEOODLY BLAT BAP WEEDLY WOP.'

I've heard a guitar run that was not only fast, and I mean *fast*, but had a real Rock 'n' Roll *sound*. Now anything you experience in life that you don't believe is possible, don't register immediately. You know it happened but your brain tells you it's impossible, so it tries to blank it out. I've looked round at the guitarist, he's casually fiddling with the controls on his amp.

'Do that again,' I've said.

'What?' he said.

'What you just did.' So there he's gone again:

The Outlaws – Mick Underwood, Ke

dgren, me and Ritchie Blackmore.

I had long hair in this publicity handout but Joe Meek had it cut off to make me look 'smart'.

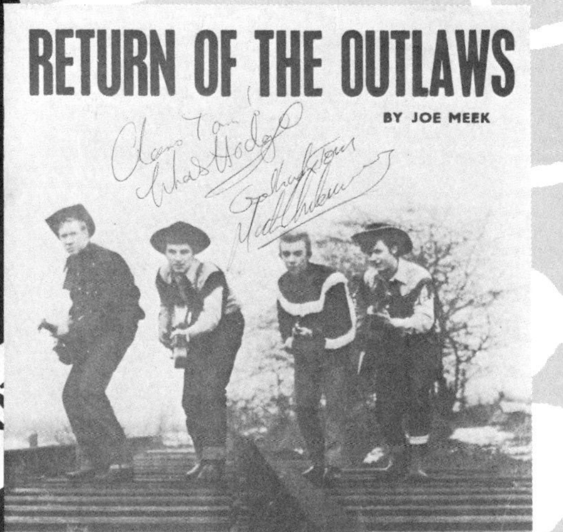

Above left Early piano playing days and early piano amplification – Mike Berry sticking vocal mike into the piano! **Above right** Mick Underwood, Ritchie (on the ground) and me buggering about. **Top** The Outlaws with our last lead guitarist, Harvey (second from the right).

'DIDDLY DIDDLY DIDDLY DIDDLY DUM BOOBABABABLAT BLAT WEEDLY WOP'

'What, that?'

'Fuck me, yer! Let's do a song, what do you know?'

I'd forgotten the piano player.

'The piano player likes Jerry Lee,' said the guitarist lookin' toward his mate who's sat there at the piano motionless lookin' like a shop window dummy that's bin on a hunger strike.

'Alright, how about "I Could Never Be Ashamed of You"' I've said, at the same time tryin' to think how I'm gonna get rid of the piano player and keep the guitarist. Bonk! We've gone into it.

The piano player from the back looks like he's not started. His body and head never moved. But, am I imaginin' it or is the most incredible noise comin' out of that piano? It can't be. He's not movin'. I've walked over to the piano. Only his hands were movin' but the sound they were makin' were Jerry Lee! My favourite Rock 'n' Roll pianist!

Now, like I said, you've got to realise that English Rock 'n' Roll musicians were new at the game. American Rock 'n' Rollers had the edge. You had to get *near* 'em before you ever thought of *overtakin'* 'em. Here were two musicians that were not only near 'em, they *topped* 'em. We've gotta have 'em! What a band we'll be!

But they never joined.

To this day I don't know why, but they didn't. Perhaps I was too enthusiastic, perhaps I should have been a bit more cool. I don't know. They stayed with Sutch. P'raps they got the hump when we said we didn't want the piano player at first and had just come down to taunt us. Anyway they didn't join but they suggested another ex-Sutch guitarist: Scratch and Scrape Bailey. No-one's gonna top that, I thought, but I was pleasantly surprised when he turned up. He wasn't as 'fast', but he had a great sound and a good Rock 'n' Roll feel. He joined The Outlaws and once more we had a workin' band. Me on bass, Biffo rhythm, Scratch lead guitar, Don on drums and Mike vocals. One of the first tours we did was Scotland. We had 'Just a Matter of Time' out which the new band was on.

Life on the road with a bunch of blokes you hardly know is always interesting, to say the least. You soon do get to know each other and have to learn to get along. It wasn't unusual for a clash of personalities to be sorted out with a punch-up. Scratch used to have digs at Biffo. Poor old Biffo. Scratch would really give Biffo stick, about how his guitar was always out of tune, and how all he liked was the 'Shads'.

We used to say to Biffo, 'Stick up for yourself. He won't let up 'til you do.' But Biffo was too easy – until one day. We was sittin' in a cafe. Scratch started on Biffo again. Right out of the blue (and we all sat back in amazement) Biffo said, 'Say one more word, Scratch, and I'll punch you straight on the fuckin' nose.' Well done, Biffo! Scratch was struck dumb. He made an attempt at a joke, lookin' towards us for support, got none and bottled out. Biffo got no more trouble from Scratch. Scratch became a nicer bloke after that and we all got on better. But Scratch *was* to get a punch on the nose, only not from Biffo.

We were on stage somewhere in the middle of Scotland, setting up for a sound check. Mike Berry was in a bad mood about something, I can't remember what. Anyway he came stormin' on to the stage, said something to Scratch, Scratch called him a cunt, and Wallop! Mike had turned round about three times with his fist stuck out, caught Scratch on the jaw and sent him flying off the stage to the middle of the dance floor. I was shocked to see poor old Scratch flyin' through the air. He wore glasses and was littler than Mike. I leapt at Mike and pushed him.

'What did you fuckin' do that for? He didn't deserve that,' I said.

Mike immediately felt guilty and we jumped down to see how Scratch was. His glasses were all bent up, and all he kept sayin' was, 'I'll fuckin' get you, Berry.'

We straightened his glasses out as best we could while Mike was trying to apologise. But Scratch didn't want to know.

'I'll fuckin' get you, Berry,' was all he kept sayin'.

That night Scratch's face blew up like a football. The next day it was worse. We took him down the hospital, they x-rayed his jaw and found it was broken. They had to wire it up and he spent the rest of the tour like that, drinking soup. Mike had exhausted his apologies but every now and then Scratch would say through his wired-up teeth, which made it sound even more threatening, 'I'll fuckin' get you, Berry.'

He never did, but Mike feels guilty to this day. So you should, you big bully!

Biffo was the first one to leave that band. Scratch suggested as a replacement a Canadian bloke he knew. Ken Lundgren. Ken was to become a big mate of mine and still is. Apart from bein' good on the guitar (and steel guitar) Ken was good at organising things. This was what we needed. Ken drove the van (on the wrong side of the road at first!), rang agents, fixed gigs and did just about everything, and drank like a fish. I liked a couple of pints but I wasn't in Ken's class. We'd be drivin' home from a gig in the ol' Thames van. Ken'd have a crate o' beer beside him to 'keep me awake'. I'd be behind him with a rolled-up road map ready to whack him on the back of the head when he started nodding off, which was often. Poor ol' Ken was the only one who had a licence to drive.

The Outlaws were now doing a lot of gigs on their own. We were becoming less available to back Mike Berry on his gigs so he left to form his own backing band. With Ken as the new rhythm guitarist we recorded 'Sioux Serenade' and 'Ku-Pow'. We spent about six months on the road with this line-up. The next one to go was Scratch. He announced one day, right out of the blue, that he was going to emigrate to Australia, on his own.

A lead guitar player was needed, so we did the auditioning bit. No good. None of 'em was as good as *I* was on the guitar. Perhaps this was the answer. It might be easier to find a bass player and I go on lead guitar. I liked playin' either instrument so it didn't matter to me. I suggested it to Joe Meek (it was at Joe's place we'd bin holding the auditions). Joe thought it was a great idea.

'I know a bass player who came up from Southampton with a group to audition,' Joe said. 'I think we could get him.'

'What's he like?'

'Well, he's tall, quite good lookin'.'

'No, you prat, what's he like on the *bass?*' Trust Joe!

'I'll get him down and see what you think of him.' He turned up. His name was Heinz Burt.

I wasn't impressed. He was a bit image-conscious, to say the least. Not a very desirable quality for a musician to have, in my book. I hoped he was goin' to be useless. It would have made it easier. As it happens he weren't too bad, but he didn't fit in. He was too ambitious. No good for us. We didn't want to be stars if it meant pandering to the masses. We wanted to enjoy ourselves and play good music and fuck about and that. I decided to take the easy way out and rather than tell Joe I didn't like him, I told Joe I didn't think *I* was up to playing lead guitar and I wanted to go back on bass.

'Okay,' said Joe. 'We'll carry on auditioning for a lead guitarist. But I shall build a band round Heinz.'

By this time Don Groom had got fed up and skint hangin' around while we found someone. He went off to join Mike Berry's new group, The Innocents. We now needed a drummer as well as a lead guitarist. The advert went back in the *Melody Maker,* now saying, 'Drummer and Lead Guitarist wanted for Hit Recording Artists, The Outlaws'. Things were looking gloomy. But every cloud has a silver lining. I got a phone call from someone who had been up at Joe Meek's.

'I've just seen Alan Caddy and Clem Cattini (Johnny Kidd's guitarist and drummer) walk into Joe Meek's to audition for The Outlaws.'

Great! I'd heard them play. Perfect! I've rang Joe.

'Is it true?'

'Yes,' said Joe. 'But they're no good for you so I'm forming a group with them round Heinz.'

'But I know how they play. I *like* 'em.'

'Well, they're now in my new group I'm forming called The Tornadoes.'

Fanks, Joe!

We carried on auditioning. We found a drummer who suited us. Mick Underwood. All we needed was a lead guitarist. Me and Ken remembered seeing a guitar player (another one who was with Sutch) that we liked. Let's find out what he's up to. We found out his name was Ritchie Blackmore and we got him down. He wasn't particularly quick at pickin' up a tune but he had a style of his own, a good sound and a good Rock 'n' Roll feel. He was in.

Chapter 10
Jerry Lee Lewis Tour

The new Outlaws had fire. Me, Ken, Mick Underwood and Ritchie were a Rock 'n' Roll band to be reckoned with. Right. All we need is gigs to prove ourselves and we're away. Someone saw in one of the music papers that Gene Vincent was looking for a backing group. Ken got on the phone. Don Arden came down with Gene Vincent to have a look at us, liked us, and we got the job. The tour that was coming up was a tour with Jerry Lee. Fantastic! On the same bill as Jerry Lee! I'll get to meet the bloke. But the best was yet to come. Don Arden called us into his office a couple of days before the tour.

'Fellas, you've got a choice. Jerry Lee needs a backing group. You can back Gene Vincent or Jerry Lee.'

Got a choice? There was only one. Gene Vincent was one of my Rock 'n' Roll heroes, but Jerry Lee was God! It was too good to be true. Something had to happen to take the edge off it, and it did. Joe Meek called us into his office to announce that Heinz had now left The Tornadoes to become a star in his own right.

'Oh, great. Good luck to him.'

'He is going to be added to the Jerry Lee tour.'

Mistake, I thought, but it wasn't none of my business. I should have guessed what he was leading up to, though.

'He needs a backing group and I would like The Outlaws to back him.'

Hold up a minute. I had nothing personal against Heinz but in my books he just wasn't any good. Jerry Lee and Gene Vincent *were*. Also, his image was all wrong for the show, he was too flash.

The greasy, lary Jerry Lee and Gene Vincent followers were not gonna take kindly to the 'White Tornado'. He was a ladies' Rock 'n' Roller. His image was fashioned to appeal to the tarts. The audience we were gonna get would be 90% herberts and I didn't wanna be associated with him. No, sod that. Not under any circumstances can we back Heinz.

But they say everyone has his price, and on this occasion we were skint. On top of all that our gear was falling apart. Amps held together with gaffer tape, bass strings that had been boiled for the tenth time (a cheap way of puttin' a bit of life back in 'em), and the arses were hangin' out of our trousers.

'Look,' said Joe, sensing not a lot of enthusiasm, 'before you turn it down I would like you to meet someone.' In comes this geezer, a typical hard-lookin' businessman. He was introduced to us and we waited to see what he had to say. It was like something out of a Rock 'n' Roll film.

'Boys, I'll come straight to the point. I am a millionaire and I am to become Heinz's manager. I would like you to back Heinz on this tour. If you accept, you will each be given an open cheque book, and providing everything you spend is to the benefit of the band, you may spend as much as you like. New amplifiers, guitars, basses, drums, clothes, new van, whatever. Just make sure I get a bill for everything. You will be on a retainer of £30 a week for your food, etc. In return I shall expect 50% commission on your earnings when you become famous.'

Famous! He could have said 200% of our earnings, it wouldn't have made any difference. We never had no plans to become famous. We just wanted to enjoy ourselves, play good music and fuck about and that. *Good music!* I pulled myself together to ask an important question, my compromise.

'If we back Heinz, does it affect us backin' Jerry Lee?' Even all this I would've turned down if he'd have said it did.

'No, I see no reason why you shouldn't back Jerry Lee too.'

Great!

The next minute there we were, hoppin' up and down Charing Cross Road like we'd just bin let out of a nut house. We've gone mad! Gibson Guitars! Epiphone Bass! 12 String Guitar! Drumkit, Strings, Cases, Gibson Amps, Fender Amps! We bought the lot. Ken took time off to ring his local garage to order a new van. Every now and then it crossed my mind that the price we had to pay was having to back Heinz. But that won't be too bad. We were still backing Jerry Lee – and we had all this new gear! New amps, new guitars! It's gonna be great! I can cope. Or could I?

The show opened in Birmingham Town Hall. We'd been filming in the morning, a film called 'Live It Up' in which Heinz was starring. We arrived in Birmingham just in time for a quick run-through with Jerry Lee. We did 'Great Balls of Fire' and a couple of others, and I could tell Jerry Lee was impressed with our band. I swelled with pride!

The show started. We were to open, then Heinz, then Gene Vincent, and Jerry Lee was to close. Off we went with a few Outlaws Rock 'n' Roll tunes. We went down great. It was Heinz's turn. We announced him to the backing of 'C'mon Everybody'. The crowd waited, and so did we. Then, from off stage (this was his idea for his entrance) Heinz started singin' 'Well come on everybody.' I say singin', it sounded more like an old blow-lamp that kept goin' out. The crowd showed no emotion but waited expectantly, wondering what they were about to witness. Then a white head appeared around the corner followed by a body movin' sort of like Elvis having just shit himself.

He just about got to the centre of the stage, the crowd still quiet. Then one lone voice in the audience hollered, 'Fuck off you cunt!'

The place erupted. A hail of ice-cream cartons, beer cans and anything they could get their hands on flew towards the stage from all directions. I gotta admit I didn't help things. I sort of tried to pretend I wasn't with him. It wasn't very professional of me but I couldn't help it. You see, when I was in the role of the punter I was as bad as them and I'd holler and hoot if I didn't think the band was any good. Mind you, it was only the poser-type bands I did it to. The flash bands that had no talent. Now I was thinkin', 'If I was out there, would I look upon me as being part of a flash band?' I squirmed at the thought. I backed away from Heinz like he had the plague and joined in with the crowd. Like I said, it wasn't very professional of me and I wasn't proud of myself but I couldn't help it. I must say he had guts. He didn't let up. He went through the whole of his act, layin' on the floor and all that, but it didn't work. He was simply booked on the wrong show. He was a 'tarts' act. On some other tour he might have done okay but not this one. Gene Vincent and Jerry Lee fans were hardly the most polite bunch, even to the best support bands.

Backing Jerry Lee on that tour was fantastic. It more than made up for backing Heinz. We finished off at the Star Club in Hamburg.

Ritchie fell in love at the Star Club. Her name was Margret. I remember him saying, 'Who's that bird down the front who looks like Doris Day?' And our tour manager, Henry Henroid, saying, 'Blimey! He's well hooked, ain't he?' He was right.

Ritchie bought her an engagement ring and brought her back to England like a lot of musicians did who went to Hamburg. They all got hooked up with German birds. I think she was in the pudden club, though I can't be certain (I don't wanna get sued), but I remember the day they married alright!

It wasn't long after we all got back from Hamburg. We all went to the wedding and had to rush away to a gig in Salisbury. It had been a sort of unusual affair. Not the kind of wedding atmosphere I had been brought up with. I'd seen a few weddings in my time too. What with Great-grandfather's and Mum's. Ritchie got married and perhaps he felt different, but we all felt we'd been to a court case. Something that was our duty to do. We done it, and that was it. Now we had to get to the gig.

We were second on the bill. This new band were topping the bill. They'd just got a record in the charts. A scruffy load of jumped-up skifflers called The Rolling Stones. The place was packed. Mostly teenage girls who were there to see The Rolling Stones. We came on to do our set which normally went down a bomb, but they weren't there to see us.

Some of 'em gave us the time of day, but there was a little bunch of girls down the front who, after every number, started chanting, 'We want the Rolling Stones!' and all that.

One of the girls at the front, who was directly in line with Ritchie, was drinking a bottle of Coke through a straw. She decided it was a good idea to suck up Coke through the straw and blow it over Ritchie's trousers. Every time she hit target her mates fell about. She was having a great time. Little did she know that Margret was in the wings watching all this.

Now I could see what Ritchie meant when he likened Margret to Doris Day, but Margret was the *German* version of Doris Day. She was just a bit bigger all round, and I don't mean fat, she had muscles. I don't mean that unkindly. She told me once that a woman should take pride in the physical condition of her body. She should be fit and strong. Margret was. The girl who was blowing Coke over Ritchie's trousers (and her mates) were about to find out how strong.

The girl was sucking down her straw for the fifth go at squirting Ritchie's trousers when Margret's run onto the stage, grabbed the girl and give her a punch that sent her sprawling amongst her mates. She stood there as the girl's mates got up from the floor. Then one of 'em made a grab for Margret. She caught hold of Margret's skirt. The rest joined in but all they succeeded in doing was pulling her skirt off. Margret, now stood there in her drawers, dived off the stage in amongst the lot of 'em. And she laid into 'em! A big circle was formed and the girls who weren't flattened just run for it. The band kept playing, by the way, and though I was motioning to Ritchie to get down there and help her, he just gave me a wide-eyed and dumbstruck look. I suppose he thought, 'I'll carry on doing what I do best. She don't look as though she needs any help from me or

Jerry L

ı the Outlaws.

Jerry Lee and me.

Arriving in Germany to back Jerry Lee – only! I hope I wasn't too hard on poor old Heinz.

'Country Boy' looks like a big hit for Heinz

BUBBLING with ideas and excitement over future plans, Heinz walked proudly into the DISC office last week with a copy of his latest record "Country Boy." And it looks like following "Just Like Eddie" into the charts.

"Geoff Goddard wrote the number for me some months ago and The Saints and myself got together in the recording studio a couple of weeks ago and recorded it in one morning. Surprisingly enough, it only took about three takes before we were all happy with it."

Heinz has just had a record player fitted into his car. "It's very small and operates on the same principle as a car radio, the only difference being that I can play the records I like to hear.

"In fact, what with being constantly on the road, The Saints and I find it very useful for learning the beat and lyrics to our new numbers. Joe Meek my manager cuts a very rough demo for us and we play this as we are travelling."

The success of Heinz's hit "Just Like Eddie" has meant a lot to him. "It's gone down well wherever we've played it. The boys and I were on a show in Liverpool recently which starred, apart from us, an all-Liverpool bill.

"I felt sure that the audience would reject us, but our act got a marvellous ovation. All the Liverpool boys could say was 'We told you so.'"

Heinz is also looking forward to his trip to Sweden. "It'll probably mean that The Saints and I will not be able to spend Christmas at home but the Swedes are becoming very beat conscious and we'd love to play in their country."

Heinz is keen to travel. "The British audiances come first," he said. "But I'd like the chance to visit the States. If I ever did get over there I'd particularly like to meet the late Eddie Cochran's parents."

Heinz, dressed in a smart blue suit, left claiming that he looked scruffy. "I'm now going to blow the whole of my allowance on new clothes," he said as he left with determined steps in the direction of Oxford Street.

Tony Noakes

I could have spelt it better at the time by omitting the 'o'.

anybody.' She didn't, either. 'I spend ze morning pressing my Reechie's trousers,' she said later. 'I have no one spoilin' zem!' Quite right too.

That girl's eyes (and her mates') must water to this day every time she hears a Rolling Stones record. Those around her might think she's weeping through nostalgia. But those who know, know better.

We did the odd gig when we came back home from the Star Club but we were shortly to go on the road with Gene Vincent. He lived in England and needed a backing group to tour Britain. Jerry Lee had gone back home so this was most definitely the next best thing. I was looking forward to it.

Chapter 11
Gene Vincent

Poor old Gene Vincent. I liked Gene. He was a bit mixed-up and used to annoy a few people he worked with, but once you got to know Gene you realised it was all front. He couldn't handle the 'being a star' bit. Then again, when he'd fallen from favour, he couldn't handle that, either. He liked a laugh, though, when he was in one of his better moods. Deep down I think he just wanted to be one of the boys.

The first time we backed Gene I was thrilled. Even more so when he came up to me after the gig and asked me personally if I'd go with him to Geneva. He couldn't take the whole band but would I go with him to show the resident Swiss band the chords and routine, etc.

'They absolutely love me over there,' he said. 'They actually roll out the red carpet when I arrive. I am treated like God! Of course, if you're with me you'll get the same treatment.'

Fantastic! I thought. Unbelievable! One of my Rock heroes wants *me* as right-hand man. I'm there like a shot.

'We've got to leave at 6 am for the airport,' says Gene. 'It'll be best if you stay at my flat so's we're ready to go. What have you got to wear? Have you got a suit? Never mind, I'll sort you out one of mine.' I'd not long been courting at the time (I was going out with this girl called Joan). I dropped a note round her house after that night's gig, telling her that Gene Vincent's asked me to go to Geneva with him, so I couldn't see her that night. (She's still got this note, incidentally.) I went straight on round to Gene's house. Me and Gene sat up all night. I was fascinated by his stories and also a bit wary every now and then when he went into things like, 'You know, I shot a man in Rochester?' And staring at me with his big bally eyeballs.

'Oh yer, Gene. Whatever happened to Cliff Gallup?' (The guitarist on Gene's hits.)

Cockin' a deaf 'un, he'd get his collection of Nazi armbands and guns out. Then he'd put 'em all away and drag me into his bedroom to show me his new-born baby, and gettin' a bollockin' from his missus. I thought this was out of order – the bollockin' I mean. I mean, you can't say to that famous Rock 'n' Roller, Gene Vincent, 'Why don't you stop makin' so much noise and bugger off to bed.' Can ya? 'Be-Bop-a-Lula' wasn't like this in the song.

Anyway, I've finally got me nut down about 4 am. An hour later, Gene's woke me up with a light ale and a suit on a hanger.

'I'd sooner have a cup of tea, Gene.'

'Try this suit on, Chas,' he goes. I'm taller than Gene but I've tried the jacket on. It wasn't too bad. Sleeves was a bit too short, but passable. He's give me the trousers. They were a bit on the short side an' all, to say the least, but I buttoned up the jacket and worked 'em down a bit. Not bad at all. At least it's a suit. Red carpet! Geneva! Gene Vincent's personal arranger! I'm getting excited.

At 5 o'clock I'm ready to go. Guitar, clean shirts, passport. I'm ready. Gene's ready. Suitcase, crutches, half a bottle of Scotch. 'Bang', there's a knock on the door.

'Gene!' I've heard, in one of the loudest voices I'd *ever* heard.

'It's Don,' says Gene. He opens the door. Don walks in. Gene's manager.

'Come on, Gene. Put the Scotch back in the cupboard, we've got half an hour to catch the plane.'

Gene waddles out to the car. I'm right behind him carryin' me gear. Ignoring me completely, Don Arden's said to Gene, 'Who's he?'

'Well Don,' says Gene, 'I thought, Geneva. Strange Band. I thought, well p'raps they won't know the tunes, I just thought . . . '

'I *told* you Gene. *No* musicians! Band's laid on. They know your act better than you do. Now come on, get in.' Gene's got in without so much as a 'See ya' to me. Don's got in and they're away. I'm left standin' there in the middle of some mews in the West End, guitar in one hand, suitcase in the other, lookin' like Norman Wisdom in Gene Vincent's poxy suit. The car's disappeared round the corner. Good ol' Gene! I got *your* number.

Nevertheless we ended up backin' him on the road. Lookin' back, I enjoyed it. He could be a nuisance sometimes, but deep down he was alright. He'd say things like, 'You know, Chas, 'Be-Bop-a-Lula' sold three million records.' Lookin' at you with his great big bally eyeballs.

'Did it, Gene? I really loved that record.' I did too.

'You don't believe me?' I *did* believe him. 'I'm telling you, Chas, I earned a fortune out of that song!'

I *believed* him! 'I believe you Gene, it was a great record.' I meant it.

'Chas, *I'm telling you that record sold three million copies!* How much do you think I earned out of that record, then? Peanuts? What would *you* expect to get from a three-million selling record?'

'Oh bollocks, Gene, I'm fucked if I know,' I've gone, wearying of the subject.

'Certainly not peanuts, Chas, I'm telling you!'

Am I goin' mad? How can anybody start an argument when you're agreeing with him? Gene Vincent could!

When he wanted he could put on a fantastic show. He had a unique talent. Trouble was, he had a frustrating habit of not using it when you really wanted him to. We went back to the Star Club, Hamburg with Gene in November 1963. (Cliff Bennett was there at the time. That's when I got to know him.) The first night was absolutely packed solid. The place was heaving. Half an hour before we were due on the Germans were chanting 'Zheen Wincent! Zheen Wincent!' The Outlaws have gone on, done a couple of numbers and we've announced Gene. The roof's lifted off as Gene's waddled on. I'm glowin'! Go on, Gene, give it to 'em! I can't wait.

Our cue to start was 'Be-Bop-a-Lula, She's My Baby'. Snare drum beat and all in. Gene's stood still in the middle of the stage, dodgy leg stuck out, clutching the mike, the crowd's gone quiet waitin' for *it.* We're excited, waiting for the 'Be-Bop-a-Lula' cue. But it don't come. Gene decides to have a little chat to 'em instead.

'Ah bin havin' some trouble with mah leg. Ah don't suppose ya all know but ah first broke it in a motor bike accident and then ah broke it again in a car crash when mah poor friend Eddie Cochran died. Ah've had a new plaster put on this week and ah've bin told by the doctors ah've got to exercise it. But *they* don't know! *They* don't know the *pain* ah'm in!'

The Deutschers are just standin' there silent. They just want to rock 'n' roll. But Gene's turned to us and said, 'I think for a change tonight, fellas, we'll kick off with a song I recorded a few years back, 'Lavender Blue'. Gimme a chord.'

Plang! 'Lavender Blue, dilly dilly . . .'

The crowd sort of looked let down. 'Gene,' I think to myself, 'I don't think they really wanted you to do "Lavender Blue".'

But then we'd go to some little Corn Exchange gig where nobody hardly took any notice and Gene would pull it out of the bag. Also, I soon found out that Gene would put on a great show if he knew an old mate had come to see him. One of his best shows was when Johnny Kidd turned up one night. Gene had that way about him. *He* decided when to put on a good show.

Gene was with us on the road towards the end of our Flour Bag Throwin' era. We got the idea a few months earlier when we were on tour with The Saints who were now backin' Heinz. Our vans would follow each other from gig to gig. We both had vans that had sliding doors. We'd stop at cafes together, jump back in our vans together, overtake each other, slide back the doors and chuck things. I think it was Ritchie Blackmore who hit on the brilliant idea of buying bags of flour and throwin' 'em from the van at people we passed. I know Ritchie was the best shot. It's not easy to hit a movin' target when you're movin' even faster in the opposite direction, but Ritchie could, almost every time.

We'd make a small split in the bags. This made sure of the desired effect on impact. It was every bit as good as you imagined it would be. Clouds and clouds of flour! We picked our victims carefully. No old people or kids. The perfect victim was a cocky geezer who thought he was *it*, dressed up to go out for a night with the boys. The sort of bloke that would murder you if he got hold of you, but that added to the excitement. Those boring long journeys (before there were many motorways) were now looked upon in a different light. The longer the journey, the more fun we were going to have. We'd have a whip round before the set off, arm ourselves with a cardboard box full of flour bags and off we'd go. This particular day, Gene was with us in the van. We knew he liked a laugh and couldn't wait to show him the Flour Bag Throwin' bit. We were goin' to Swansea in the days before the M4. Normally that journey would be moaned about, but now we had flour bags we could chuck.

We had the whip-round and with a big box full of flour bags we set off. We threw them at herberts all up the A4. Through towns and villages we left a trail of flour. Gene loved it. Sometimes the aim wasn't too accurate and the bag would burst on the edge of the van door or something. The inside of the van was white, we were white and we were enjoying ourselves. As we neared Swansea, we spotted a perfect target. Some geezer had broken down at the side of the road. He had his bonnet up and his head in it. As we drove past, Wallop! We dropped a flour bag on his head. We fell about. The engine must have been runnin' and the fan gave out a nice effect! The whole car was obliterated byclouds of flour. As we were lookin' through the back window of the van, havin' hysterics, we saw through the haze the man slam down his bonnet and jump in his car. He was off after us. In seconds he was *on* us. He drew up alongside and leaned out. His face was a picture. Pure white with a big bushy beard that was the same colour! He aimed a fuckin' great brick at us. 'Doiyng!' It hit the side of the van and we put our foot down. Gene was lookin' worried! We did lefts and rights and detours and after about four or five miles we managed to lose him. We finally arrived at the gig on the outskirts of Swansea, still laughin'. We were early and couldn't get in, so we sat there waitin' for someone to turn up.

Someone did. But it wasn't the manager of the gig. It was the flour-bag victim! He'd been determined to catch us and he had. He parked his motor and walked over to our van. He looked like a statue that had come to life.

'Oi, cunt!' he said to Gene who was sittin' in the passenger seat. 'You bin slingin' flour bags about?'

'No, Sir!' said Gene in his polite Southern manner.

'Don't fuckin' "No Sir" me!' he said. He stuck his head in the van window. There we all were. The inside of the van was white and so were we. He was wild but p'raps, seeing all us lot in there, changed his mind about punching Gene.

'I happen to think it ain't very funny,' he said. 'You ain't heard the last of this.'

He was right too. He reported us to the police and we ended up gettin' nicked for it. We had to go to court somewhere along the A4. We had no insurance or tax at the time so we really got the book thrown at us. He got his own back alright. We had to cut out the flour-bag throwin' from then on. It was a shame and we missed it, but we couldn't chance gettin' nicked again 'cos we still weren't insured. Y'see, no-one would insure young musicians to drive, unless you paid a fortune, so we just left it.

By this time the 'Heinz management' deal was over. We abused it rotten, generally fucked about and enjoyed ourselves. Heinz's manager had enough of us and dropped us. We still kept the gear, though. The flour-bag era was over, but we did have a little fling with catapults and goosegogs . . .

Once again, Gene was in the van. We'd stopped at a level crossing. Some bird walked past the van with one of them Sixties PVC macs on. The old catapult was loaded. 'Wop!' A goosegog hit her right in the middle of the back. It couldn't have hurt her, 'cos it made too much noise. The baggy mac took the impact. It sounded like an old slack bass drum, but she was mad! She flew at poor Gene (he always had the best seat, the passenger seat), grabbed hold of him and started shakin' him. He looked round for help.

'Leave him alone,' someone said. 'He's got a bad leg.' She's let go and started laying into him verbally. The crossing gates opened and 'Zoom!' Off we went. Gene told that story to everyone. He thought it was great. 'Wup! it went,' he'd say. Then he'd go into the flour-bag stories.

Gene would tell us stories about when he was a kid in Virginia. He said they used to have a favourite trick of findin' a fresh bit of dog shit, placing it on someone's doorstep with some newspaper over the top, set light to the newspaper and knock at the door and run away. The first thing the bloke did on openin' the door was see the burnin' newspaper and stamp on it to put it out, look around to find out who done it, see no-one and go back indoors to tread dog shit all up his passage.

Cliff Gallup, the guitar player on 'Be-Bop-a-Lula', 'Race With the Devil', etc., never went on the road with Gene. He was under the thumb, so Gene said, and cried when he left the band. Johnny Meeks, the guitar player who took his

Gene and me.

Early publicity shot of

incent – note the leg in plaster.

place, was Gene's big mate on the road.

I nearly got Gene to sing on a Heads Hands And Feet record years later. it was when we were recording 'Warmin' Up the Band'. There was a line in it that went, 'Be-Bop-a-Lula tonight, Oh Mama, yer alright.' We were recording at Advision Studios and I knew, just round the corner at the Marquee, Gene Vincent was advertised to do a gig. I said to Tony Colton (singer with H, H and F): 'Why don't I go round and bring Gene back to sing the line "Be-Bop-a-Lula?" I know he'll do it.' Tony thought it was a good idea, and off I went. Outside the Marquee was a notice. 'Owing to circumstances beyond our control Gene Vincent will not be appearing here tonight.' Apparently he was in trouble with wife maintenance and had buggered off back to America. A few weeks later he was dead. I read in the paper one morning he died of burst ulcers.

The end of another era.

Chapter 12

The Outlaws v The Beatles

We were Gene's backing band for about eight months, though through this period we were still doing our own Outlaws gigs and had built up a following. I can't remember how we split from Gene. I think we just drifted apart and went on the road as The Outlaws. Although we didn't have any hit records, the following we had was enough to pack out most gigs and we were earning money. I think that band would have made it big if it hadn't been for another band coming along to change the whole music scene. What band? The Beatles.

We'd worked with The Beatles earlier when we were backing Mike Berry. We did a week at The Cavern in Liverpool. I think it was 1962. The first time I saw their name was on posters advertising another act. The poster would advertise the act and in brackets underneath would be written '(Beatles style group)'. I mean, these bands were selling themselves on the fact that they were *like* the Beatles. So what were the *real* Beatles like? The first I saw of 'em was at a gig in Bootle. Mike Berry and The Outlaws were topping the bill, The Beatles were second. We sat and watched 'em. We were reasonably impressed at the time, but weren't *mad* on 'em.

Back in the dressing-room, I was talking to 'em. I was talking to George. The door burst open and these birds came barging in waving autograph books. I stood up reachin' for me pen. They've screamed, but not 'Eeeeeeek, The Outlaws!' but 'Eeeeeeek, The Beatles!' They've grabbed George, ignored me then run off to the rest of 'em, ignoring the rest of us. I put me pen away.

But The Outlaws, me, Ken, Mick Underwood and Ritchie were still doing okay. The Beatles had had a bit of a hit with 'Love Me Do', which I thought wasn't a bad record but no threat. The Outlaws were still packin' 'em in. I remember one gig in particular where we couldn't go wrong. It was in Stourbridge and was run by Fred Bannister (who promoted Knebworth many years later). We'd arrive and there'd be queues outside the door. We were the Kings! But on one of our return bookings we've arrived. No queue! Our first thought was, 'There's been a mix-up, and we've turned up on the wrong night.' But no. *There* were the posters. 'Outlaws, appearing by public demand. Here tonight.' Public demand? What public, where are they? We've gone round the pub and got back to the dressing-room about half an hour before we were due on. The hall *must* be packed by now. They probably all turned up while we were round the pub. We sneaked a look through the curtains. No more than two dozen people stood round the stage waitin' for us to go on. Something's definitely wrong, we thought, bad advertising or something, I mean they're usually spilling out the doors. Anyway, let's go and do our bit.

The two dozen fans did their best to make us feel at home, but we had to get to the bottom of this. A few of 'em came back after to see us. 'Where is everybody?' we said. 'They've gone to see The Beatles. They're on down the road,' they said.

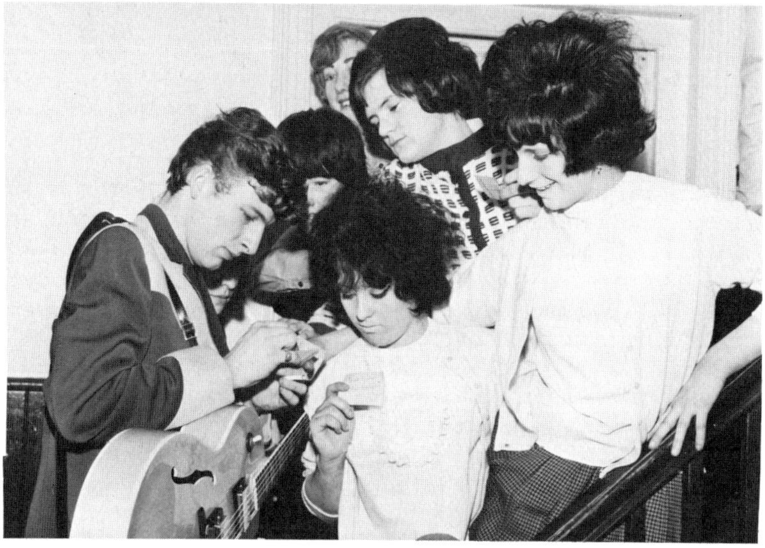

I think these were the only five who came to see us in Stourbridge. The other 500 went down the road to see the new band, The Beatles.

The Beatles. That band again!

Well, The Beatles were on their way and ya don't need me to tell ya how their career progressed from there. But The Outlaws' career moved just as quickly as theirs. In the opposite direction. Everyone started to panic. Change this, change that. I thought we should have carried on regardless but I was outvoted. It was the 'Liverpool Sound' now. Dave Clark had got away with it, so Joe Meek thought, 'Why not The Outlaws?' But it was outside of Joe's mode of thinking. He should have stuck to his guns too. At least he knew what he was doing in his own field. I mean, The Beatles were alright. Their songs were good but we could *play* better than them. But Joe began asking us how the Liverpool groups got that *sound*. Joe couldn't make it out. They sounded like rough demos. But they were getting into the charts.

A half-hearted version of 'Shake With Me' was our attempt at the Liverpool Sound. We didn't like it. The other side, which was more us, was our consolation for letting that record out. It was 'Keep-a-Knockin'. The solo Ritchie did on it was good. He got the idea from a solo Bernie Watson (the almost-Outlaw with the 'Diddly-Diddly' licks) had done on a Sutch record. Sutch's band had done some good stuff for Joe Meek. Ritchie took the idea and improved on it. Ritchie, as I said, didn't have a particularly good 'ear' for music. You'd sing him a line that he had to play, and he was ages getting it off. But he was good in other ways. He had a good sound and a good technique. The solo he did on 'Keep-a-Knockin' was wild, but effective. But, apart from stories later that it was one of Jimmy Hendrix's favourite guitar solos, it went unnoticed and the band became disillusioned and skint. Ritchie left to join another band. I think he went to Germany. We needed a guitarist once more.

We got hold of Harvey Hinsley who became another good mate of mine. He's with Hot Chocolate now. We went back on the road and had some fun but never made no money. The final straw was Ken Lundgren announcing he was goin' back to Canada. We got hold of Ed Hamilton to take his place and did a few gigs, but they got less and less. The spark wasn't there. The Outlaws were doomed. We split up and went our own ways. No more Outlaws.

I did a few gigs here and there. A couple of sessions with Derek Lawrence (a producer who much later gave me and Dave a free hand to do our 'One Fing an' Anuvver' album) helped me to survive, just. I started doing some demos with Micky Tinsley, or Micky Dallon as he's known in the pop world. I'd first met Micky at the King's Head. He'd got a songwriting deal with some company, and me and him would put down on tape demos of his songs. Mick was a character and had a good sense of humour.

I didn't earn much from that episode, but learnt a lot and developed my talent for recording ideas. I was always interested in tape recorders and editing and overdubbing and that. Mick on my suggestion got hold of two Ferrograph tape recorders. I'd overdub between the two tapes – piano, guitar and whatever – then we'd add vocals. The demos we turned out were good.

Mick liked the glamour side of the pop world. I wasn't too interested in that. I was just into the music, but all the same Mick, being a bit of a snappy dresser, came in handy one night.

I was round his house bungin' down a demo. We'd finished and I was about to go home. It was pourin' down with rain, I hadn't a coat to my name, but Mick's wardrobe was full of coats (or so he led everyone to believe).

'Do you wanna borrow a coat, Chas?'

'Cheers, Mick.'

Mick's come back with a coat. A sort of Executive Producer's special. Furry collar and the rest, made out of trendy nylon. Not quite me, but it was rainin'.

'Take care of it, Chas.'

'Sure, Mick. I'll let you have it back tomorrow.'

Tomorrow never came. Like I said, I wasn't mad on the style of it, but coats keep you warm. I kept wearing it. It soon got wore in. A couple of fag holes appeared down the front, the fur got chewed by our dog Mitch, and the linin' started to come adrift.

Mick kept asking me, 'Where's my bleedin' mac?'

'I put it in the cleaners, Mick.'

I was just putting it off hoping he'd forget about it. I couldn't possibly give it back to him now. Once I knew it had gone so far, I lost interest in keepin' it in good nick. I wore it everywhere. Fishin', up the pub, in the garden. I meant to get it cleaned but I was kiddin' myself. It was too late. Mick still kept asking about his mac and I kept saying 'It's still in the cleaners, I'll bring it tomorrow.' In the end Mick got fed up askin' and I forgot about it, until, well, it wasn't really *my* fault.

I didn't even know how it got there. Where? I'll tell you.

Mick's come round one night, the mac subject now forgotten. We're talking about a new song, how it should be done, etc, etc. Mick's got up to leave

THE JOE MEEK HIT PARADE

Here is a list of all the RGM Productions which reached the Top 50

Artist / Title	Label	YEAR	H/P
BERRY, Mike &the Outlaws			
TRIBUTE TO BUDDY HOLLY	HMV POP 9I2	I96I	I9
DON'T YOU THINK IT'S TIME	HMV POP II05	I963	4
MY LITTLE BABY	HMV POP II42	I963	3I
CHAKIRIS, George			
HEART OF A TEENAGE GIRL	Triumph RGM I0I0	I960	49
CHARLES, Don			
WALK WITH ME MY ANGEL	DECCA FII424	I962	34
COX, Micheal			
ANGELA JONES	Triumph RGM I0II	I960	7
ALONG CAME CAROLINE	HMV POP 789	I960	20
CRYIN' SHAMES			
PLEASE STAY	DECCA FI2340	I966	24
DOWLANDS			
ALL MY LOVING	ORIOLE CB I897	I964	33
FLEE-REKKERS			
GREEN JEANS	TRIUMPH RGM I008	I960	22
GREGORY, Iain			
TIME WILL TELL	PYE Int. 7n I5295	I960	I8
CAN'T YOU HEAR THE BEAT OF A BROKEN HEART	PYE 7n I5397	I962	37
HEINZ			
JUST LIKE EDDIE	DECCA FII693	I963	5
COUNTRY BOY	DECCA FII768	I963	26
YOU WERE THERE	DECCA FII83I	I964	28
PLEASE LITTLE GIRL	DECCA FII920	I964	33
QUESTIONS I CAN'T ANSWER	COLUMBIA DB 7374	I964	25
DIGGIN' MY POTATOES	COLUMBIA DB 7482	I965	43
HONEYCOMBS			
HAVE I THE RIGHT	PYE 7n I5664	I964	I
IS IT BECAUSE	PYE 7n I5705	I964	29
SOMETHING BETTER BEGINNING	PYE 7n I5827	I965	38
THAT'S THE WAY	PYE 7n I5890	I965	I2
JAY, Peter & the Jaywalkers			
CAN CAN '62'	DECCA FII53I	I963	3I
LEYTON, John			
JOHNNY REMEMBER ME	TOP RANK Jar 577	I96I	I
WILD WIND	TOP RANK Jar 585	I96I	2
SON THIS IS SHE	HMV POP 956	I96I	I2
LONE RIDER	HMV POP 992	I962	38
LONELY CITY	HMV POP I0I4	I962	I4
DOWN THE RIVER NILE	HMV POPI054	I962	40
CUPBOARD LOVE	HMV POP II22	I963	22
I'LL CUT YOUR TAIL OFF	HMV POP II75	I963	36
BEAUTIFUL DREAMER	HMV POP I230	I963	29
MOONTREKKERS			
NIGHT OF THE VAMPIRE	PARLOPHONE R 48I8	I96I	37
OUTLAWS			
SWINGIN' LOW	HMV POP 844	I96I	46
AMBUSH	HMV POP 877	I96I	42

Me and The Outlaws played on most of these and even more of the flops!

Ken quits the group to go home to Canada. Going home party round Mum's. **Top** Ken, me, Harvey, Mick Underwood. **Above** Me, Joan, Linda (now Ken's wife) and Ken.

at the end of the evening.

'I must have a slash 'fore I go, Chas.'

'Alright, Mick, you know where it is.'

I've carried on strumming my guitar. 'Fore I know what's happened, Mick's back in the front room, holding up something that resembled a reject from the rag man. My heart stopped as I recognised it.

'Is this my bleedin' mac?' Mick's gone. I didn't know where to put my face! Especially after all those lies about 'in the cleaners' and that. Mick took it well. He'd found it in the bathroom. As he was havin' a slash he was talkin' to Mitch the dog who was kippin' in the bath. Mitch's bed looked familiar. It slowly dawned on Mick it was his bleedin' mac!

By now I was courting seriously, and me and Joan were engaged to be married. I was doing a few gigs here and there, though nothing positive was happenin'. But me and Joan were a happy optimistic couple, still are and always will be. We knew something would turn up, and it did. I remember saying to Joan, and I remember exactly where I was at the time. We were walkin' down Brettenham Road, Edmonton, goin' for a drink. I said, 'D'you know who my favourite band is? Cliff Bennett and The Rebel Rousers. I got to know them in Hamburg. They are great!'

Chapter 13
Cliff Bennett and The Rebel Rousers

A couple of days later I got a phone call. It was Cliff Bennett! Their bass player, Bobby Thompson, was leavin' to join The Rockin' Berries. Cliff had watched me with The Outlaws in Hamburg, and liked my style.

'Do you want the job?'

Did I! My favourite band!

I'd had offers to join other bands that were earning good money, but the music didn't suit me. Cliff Bennett and The Rebel Rousers were not only my favourite group, but they were earning good money too. What more could you wish for? They'd just had a hit, 'One Way Love', and were managed by Brian Epstein, The Beatles' manager.

I'd passed the *band's* audition, but then I had to be interviewed by NEMS (Brian Epstein's company) before I could say I was finally in. Bennett suggested I get a haircut before I go 'cos the band's image was 'smart'. I bought some 'thinning-out' scissors and give meself a haircut. That and a new pair of trousers from Johnnies Bazaar and off I went. It was like being interviewed for a job as a salesman or something. I was looked up and down, asked questions, and told I'd got the job but I must get a haircut. I didn't know what they meant by that! But I was in.

My appearance always did leave a bit to be desired. I start off with the right intentions, pressing my trousers and all that, but no matter how careful I am, I always seem to spill something down 'em and I think, 'Sod it. Ya can't spend your life worrying about how you look. There are more important things to worry about.' I knew anyway that, once I was in, musicianship and enthusiasm would hold the job down.

The Rebel Rousers were a bunch of bastards, but a good band. As I was the youngest member they gave me some stick, and I soon learnt to fend for myself. After a while, we all got on alright, after a fashion. Cliff really held the band together. He made us work and the band stayed good because of it. They were a 'drinking band' alright. I liked a drink but I was a teetotaller compared to that lot.

The line-up when I joined was: Cliff on vocals, Mick Burt drums (he's me and Dave's drummer now. I don't think of *you*, Mick, as being one of the 'bunch of bastards' but as part of the 'drinking band', well, you have been known to fit in there!), me on bass, Roy Young keyboards, Dave Wendells guitar, and Sid Phillips and Moss Groves on saxes.

Discipline was high in the band and anyone who couldn't maintain it soon got their cards. Dave Wendells was the first to go. He got the sack for being drunk and incapable. Instead of replacing him with another guitarist, Cliff talked Roy into getting a Hammond Organ. Roy wasn't too happy with the idea and was even less happy when he ended up getting one, 'cos no bleeder would

new MUSICAL EXPRESS

WORLD'S LARGEST CIRCULATION OF ANY MUSIC PAPER–WEEKLY SALES EXCEED 275,000 (MEMBERS OF ABC)

No. 947 EVERY FRIDAY PRICE 6d. March 5, 1965 Registered at the G.P.O. as a Newspaper

BEATLES FILMING by Brian Epstein

Sensational New Disc I CRY ALONE JACKIE LEE on DECCA F.12068

K.P.M. 21 DENMARK STREET W.C.2 TEM 3856

HAROLD DAVISON AND ARTHUR HOWES present

TAMLA-MOTOWN

THE FABULOUS! SUPREMES

THE EXCITING MARTHA AND THE VANDELLAS

THE FANTASTIC STEVIE WONDER

SMOKEY ROBINSON AND THE MIRACLES

EARL VAN DYKE SIX

SPECIAL GUEST STAR GEORGIE FAME AND THE BLUEFLAMES

YOUR COMPERE — TONY MARSH

FINSBURY PARK, Astoria	Sat.,	Mar. 20th,	6.40 & 9.10
HAMMERSMITH, Odeon	Sun.,	Mar. 21st,	6.00 & 8.30
BRISTOL, Colston Hall	Tue.,	Mar. 23rd,	6.30 & 8.45
CARDIFF, Capitol	Wed.,	Mar. 24th,	6.00 & 8.30
BIRMINGHAM, Odeon	Thur.,	Mar. 25th,	6.45 & 9.00
KINGSTON, A.B.C.	Fri.,	Mar. 26th,	6.45 & 9.00
BOURNEMOUTH, Winter Gardens	Sat.,	Mar. 27th,	6.00 & 8.30
LEICESTER, Odeon, Queens St.	Sun.,	Mar. 28th,	5.40 & 8.00
MANCHESTER, Odeon	Tue.,	Mar. 30th,	6.15 & 8.45
LEEDS, Odeon	Wed.,	Mar. 31st,	6.20 & 8.40
GLASGOW, Odeon	Thur.,	Apr. 1st,	6.40 & 9.00
STOCKTON, A.B.C.	Fri.,	Apr. 2nd,	6.15 & 8.30
NEWCASTLE, City Hall	Sat.,	Apr. 3rd,	6.30 & 8.45
LIVERPOOL, Empire	Sun.,	Apr. 4th,	5.40 & 8.00
LUTON, A.B.C.	Tue.,	Apr. 6th,	6.30 & 8.45
CHESTER, A.B.C.	Wed.,	Apr. 7th,	6.15 & 8.30
SHEFFIELD, City Hall	Thur.,	Apr. 8th,	6.20 & 8.50
WIGAN, A.B.C.	Fri.,	Apr. 9th,	6.20 & 8.35
WOLVERHAMPTON, Gaumont	Sat.,	Apr. 10th,	6.30 & 8.40
IPSWICH, Gaumont	Sun.,	Apr. 11th,	5.30 & 8.00
PORTSMOUTH, Guildhall	Mon.,	Apr. 12th,	6.30 & 8.50

ARTHUR HOWES presents

The World's Greatest Hit Maker

ROY ORBISON AND THE CANDYMEN

RECORDERS OF THE HIT "HE'S IN TOWN"

THE ROCKIN' BERRIES

THE SENSATIONAL ! MARIANNE FAITHFULL

THE GLAMOROUS THREE QUARTERS

YOUR COMPERE FRANK BERRY A.T.V.'s 'NIGHT SPOT'

JON MARK

EXCITING BEAT SOUND OF THE UNTAMED

CLIFF BENNETT AND THE REBEL ROUSERS

EDINBURGH, A.B.C	Fri.,	Mar. 5th,	6.30 & 8.50
STOCKTON, A.B.C.	Sat.,	Mar. 6th,	6.15 & 8.30
TOOTING, Granada	Tue.,	Mar. 9th,	7.00 & 9.10
BEDFORD, Granada	Wed.,	Mar. 10th,	7.00 & 9.10
SOUTHAMPTON, Gaumont	Thur.,	Mar. 11th,	6.15 & 8.40
CARDIFF, Capitol	Fri.,	Mar. 12th,	6.30 & 8.50
BRISTOL, Colston Hall	Sat.,	Mar. 13th,	6.20 & 8.45
COVENTRY, Coventry Theatre	Sun.,	Mar. 14th,	6.00 & 8.30
WOLVERHAMPTON, Gaumont	Tue.,	Mar. 16th,	6.30 & 8.40
SHEFFIELD, Gaumont	Wed.,	Mar. 17th,	6.30 & 8.50
NEWCASTLE, City Hall	Thur.,	Mar. 18th,	6.30 & 8.40
BRADFORD, Gaumont	Fri.,	Mar. 19th,	6.15 & 8.40
BLACKPOOL, A.B.C.	Sat.,	Mar. 20th,	6.15 & 8.45
LIVERPOOL, Empire	Sun.,	Mar. 21st,	5.40 & 8.00

WORLD REPRESENTATION outside U.S.A. for ROY ORBISON, ARTHUR HOWES LTD.
34 GREEK STREET, LONDON, W.1, by arrangement with ACUFF-ROSE ARTISTS CORPORATION OF AMERICA

I joined the band the day after this tour finished.

help him carry it. We had one roady and he couldn't manage it on his own. Roy got it sawn in half in the end and him and the roady carried a bit each. (I did help sometimes, honest!)

That bunch of bastards introduced me to poker, too. Gambling in general, like horse racing and all that, never appealed to me, but I did get to enjoy a game of poker. I still do. Reading other people's minds, trying to work out what sort of hand they've got by the moves they made was interesting, and I paid dearly for it. But I was earning money. I saw me Mum alright and still had more than I needed. Save? Never entered my head. For the first time (or the second time if you count the Heinz management deal) I had more money than I knew what to do with.

I was rich in my books. By that I mean I didn't have to worry about money in regards to paying bills. That's being *rich!* I didn't appreciate it, though. Or p'raps I did in my own way. I just spent it, or gave it away, lent it, or it just dropped out of my pocket when I got my fags out.

I was getting something like £100 to £150 a week. In 1965 that was a *lot* of money. And of course it all had to go before next pay-day. Well, isn't that what I'd always done? It was what you *did*. You tried to last your money out 'til next pay-day, and you were usually skint by at least the day before. If you did have any money left by the time next pay-day come up, you got rid of it quick in time for your new one. Saving didn't make much sense. If you saved, you saved to enjoy it later. Sooner or later, what's the difference? I wasn't one of those kids who saved his best bit of dinner 'til last. I ate the best bit first. While it was still there. Makes sense. Who knows what's gonna happen 'fore you finish your dinner? Some bleeder might pinch it!

It wasn't long after I joined Cliff Bennett that me and Dave Peacock became mates. It's funny how fate works. If it hadn't been for Joan going away, perhaps it would never have happened.

You see, at the time there was talk about a new Playboy Club opening in Park Lane. They were advertising for six girls to go to America to learn to be Bunny Girls, and come back to work and train the girls at the Park Lane club. Joan was doing fashion modelling at the time, but the work was not too plentiful, mainly because she had morals! She went for the Playboy job and got it. I was proud of her. From 1,000 girls they picked six and Joan was one of them. I was pleased, but in another way, I've got to admit, I wasn't. I trusted her 100% but I wasn't keen on other drunken geezers trying to chat her up when I wasn't around. But I knew she could look after herself and I felt it wasn't fair to stand in her way.

She left for America around the end of 1965. I missed her like mad.

It was when I was courting Joan that I met Dave, not long before Joan went away. I always missed the last bus home after saying goodbye to Joan for the twentieth time! She lived in Enfield and me in Edmonton, about three miles away. Off I'd go, thumbin' a lift. One night, an old schoolmate pulled up. Brian Juniper. I used to have a bit of a skiffle group with Brian back at Higher Grade School. He was in a band of his own now and the bloke who was with him was his bass player, Dave Peacock. On many a night after that, they'd see me thumbin' and give me a lift home. The conversation was always music. Back at my house, I'd bring 'em in for a cup of tea and we'd play records. Dave in particular seemed to like almost everythin' I liked. Jerry Lee, George Jones, pianos, banjos, family sing-songs. Then I'd end up on the piano doing me latest Jerry Lee bit, or my Earl Scruggs bit on the banjo. A sort of bond began to form and a friendship was struck up.

When Joan went to America, me and Dave started knocking around together. He used to come to the Rebel Rousers' gigs. On my nights off, we'd go and see a band. The Cooks Ferry Inn, Edmonton was always a good bet. If we weren't there with the Rebel Rousers, there was always a band worth watching. Zoot Money's Big Roll Band, Ronnie Jones and the Nightimers, John Mayall's Blues Band with Eric Clapton or Peter Green on guitar.

Me and Dave played there one night.

It must have been the first Chas and Dave gig. We took our banjos down to 'Folk Night' at the Cooks Ferry. We went on as Stoker and Wart (nicknames from the Rebel Rousers) and did 'Grandfather's Clock'. It went down a storm! We started getting invited to parties and the playing partnership began, although we didn't realize this at the time.

The club scene was great in those days. I got to know Albert Lee from the Cooks Ferry. I had heard of him and saw him play a couple of times in the early Sixties. He had a name amongst musicians. The first thing I heard him play on was a record called 'All Of Me' by Jackie Lynton (a mate of me and Dave's now and a great character with a lot of talent). Albert's guitar playing was superb.

Me and Dave, on one of my nights off from the Rebel Rousers, decided to go down the Cooks Ferry to see Chris Farlowe. Albert was with him. We were knocked out with his guitar playing and we went up and spoke to him after the gig. It turned out that Albert loved good C & W music like George Jones and Earl Scruggs and Jimmy Bryant. It was unusual for the time. Most people took the piss out of C & W music. There was, still is, and always will be a lot of duff C & W records, but the good ones amongst 'em are gems. It's a fact that they are few and far between, but the musicians who think for themselves, and don't go by what they read, will find 'em if they look for 'em. Me and Dave had found 'em and so had Albert. We introduced Albert to a good C & W band we knew who played on the Hammersmith circuit (the Red Cow, the Clarendon and the Red Lion). They were called Jamie, Jon and Jerry. 'Come down and see 'em, Albert.' Albert did and became a regular sitter-inner with the band. In between Rebel Rouser gigs me and Dave spent many a good night over Hammersmith watching Albert Lee.

Around 1966, Cliff Bennett and The Rebel Rousers got offered a tour of Germany with The Beatles. We did it and it was an experience.

We opened the show. In fact Mick Burt did. We were announced one at a time and Mick came out first wavin' his sticks. Burty's claim to fame – 'Opens show for Beatles!' When The Beatles went on, they could have played 'Knees Up Mother Brown' for all the crowd knew about it. It was continual tarts screamin' from start to finish. But they'd paid their money to enjoy theirselves and that was how they wanted to do it. By screamin' their bollocks off (well, you know what I mean).

One night The Beatles invited us to their dressing-room for a preview of their new album. As yet, it didn't have a title. A bottle of Scotch was offered toanybody who could come up with one. It ended up being called 'Revolver'. (I

Cliff Bennett, me, Moss Groves, Roy Young, Mick Burt (yes, the same!) and Sid Phillips (Sid now plays in the Chas 'n' Dave sax section).

don't know who won the bottle of Scotch.) It was still in the acetate stage. When it got to the track 'Got To Get You Into My Life', Paul said, 'Listen to this. I think it would be a good one for your band.' He was right.

Mixing with The Beatles on that tour taught me a lot. Here was a band that could pull the crowds in every country in the world. Sold literally millions of records, and yet, to hear them talk amongst themselves you'd think they'd only just started. By that I mean the 100% enthusiasm for what they'd just done, and for what they were about to do. The so-called stars I'd met before that had all acquired an air of 'Now I'm rich and famous, I must act like a "Star" and be blasé and matter-of-fact and wear car coats with hairy collars' and all that bollocks. Frightened to talk too loud about their next project, in case someone nicked it. As if anybody would! The Beatles were different. They had talent, and they knew it. They simply went out and did it. No fucking about. I never spoke to 'em a lot while we were on tour. It wasn't my style. I watched the crawlers talkin' to 'em. I just listened. About how 'Yellow Submarine' was going to be a big hit with all the little kids all over the world (they were right), about how 'Got To Get You Into My Life' was gonna be a big hit for us (they were right). About the next album, about the next gig. They never sat back and rested on their laurels.

That tour proved to me that The Beatles deserved everything they got. (They still couldn't PLAY as good as The Outlaws, though!)

When we got back to England, we went into the studio and recorded 'Got

'Got To Get You Into My Life' and I did!

Brother Dave, Joan and guess who? No, it's not me, guess again. You're right.

CONFETTI ALL THE WAY AS THE BUNNY WEDS A REBEL

SHOWERED in confetti, The Rebel and The Bunny leave church after their wedding yesterday.

The rebel: 22-year-old Chas Hodges, bass guitarist with Cliff Bennett and the Rebel Rousers pop group.

The Bunny: 20-year-old Joan Findlay, one of the six "pioneer" Bunny girls at London's Playboy Club.

Chas, (latest record, "I've Got To Get You Into My Life") married Joan at the parish church in Enfield, Middlesex.

Afterwards, at a reception, the Cliff Bennett group entertained 60 guests.

Front page news.

To Get You Into My Life'. Paul produced it and played the piano bit that leads into the solo. (He did it to cover up a duff spot.) I remember being impressed with the finished product. It sounded like a hit, and it was. Life was good. Joan had come back from America and we had made plans to get married. I had proposed. At least I thought I did. Joan said I needed a bit of egging on, but I was a bit shy in those days.

The record was in the charts when me and Joan got married. We got our picture on the front page of the *Daily Sketch*. 'REBEL ROUSER SAYS TO BUNNY GIRL "GOT TO GET YOU INTO MY LIFE"'. Dead right! I wasn't gonna let her go away again.

We moved into a flat in Cockfosters, and in 1967 our first daughter, Juliet, was born. I was a DAD! (Me and Burty had a drink on it that day in Edinburgh. Sixteen years later, me and Burty had another drink. Only this time we were in Germany. It seems to go in cycles of 16 years that I'm not home for Juliet's birthday and I'm having a drink with Mick. Where will we be in another 16 years, Mick? 1999! Summer season on the Moon? Hope there's a night porter handy!

The Rebel Rousers were still gigging, and although we didn't have any more hit records we had a good reputation and didn't need hits to earn a good living, unlike many bands then and now who are only as good as their last chart position. It was nice to have a hit but nevertheless our reputation for always being good on stage kept us in work. Socially, the band got on alright together, after a fashion! Outside of music (and poker) it was a mixture of golf and fishing.

Chapter 14

Fishing Stories

In general, when we had time off on the road, Mick, Moss and Cliff would go golfing, and me, Roy and Sid would go fishing. Me and Roy would keep our eyes open for trout streams when we were getting near to the gig or the hotel. If we spotted one that said 'Private Fishing', this was made a note of. If we had a couple of hours to spare before or after the gig then that's where we'd head. When you saw a 'Private Fishing' sign there was always a good chance of catching something. One day I caught a big 'un, and I mean a BIG 'UN!

Me, Roy and Sid all had our own individual styles of fishing. Roy was the sophisticated fisherman who reckoned he could fly fish (although I never saw him). I was the down-to-earth float fisherman, brought up on the oily canals of North London, and Sid just fucked about in general. If he never caught nothing after half an hour, he got fed up and started chucking stones in the water.

We came to a compromise in styles, though, when fishing for trout. The method we all three decided on as being best was the plastic minnow. It was about three inches long with a treble hook attached to its tail. Three hooks, welded together, with vicious points and barbs on the end of each one. Couldn't fail to hook the fish once it got hold of it. You just cast it out and wound it in, hoping a fish would be fooled and have a go at it.

Anyway, this big 'un I caught.

Me, Roy and Sid had homed in on this 'Private Fishing' trout stream. You found a likely spot, chucked your minnow out and wound it in a few times. If nothing was happening you moved on (before Sid started throwing stones in). Nothing much was happening that day so we decided to move on to another part of the stream. Off we've trooped in a line across the field. Roy leading the way, Sid next, and me behind. I've wound my little minnow in so that it dangled from the tip of my rod which I held out in front of me as we trekked across the field.

I'm looking about as I'm walking, daydreaming about catching the sort of fish that you only ever daydream about. Suddenly I've felt a tug. WALLOP! Fisherman's instinct, I've struck! 'OH! OH! OH! OH!' I've heard. It was Sid. I come back down to earth instantly to realise I'd hooked his earhole.

'What's the matter, Sid?' I said, not knowing what else to say.

'Something's stung my fuckin' earole!' said Sid. 'OH! OH! OH! OH! OOOH!'

Sid started running all round the field.

'Hold still, Sid, I'll see what it is.'

I *knew* what it was, but I didn't know how to *tell* him. I wanted to laugh but I daren't. He was bigger than me. He would have murdered me.

'I think I've hooked your earole, Sid.' I said, as casual as I could.

'OH! OH! OH! OH! GET IT OUT, GET IT OUT!'

With mixed emotions of wanting to have a laughing fit and sheer terror of what Sid might do to me, I shouted at Sid like a mum might do to a kid who's having a tantrum round the shops.

'Sid!' I hollered. 'Calm down!'

Sid stopped running round the field.

'Right,' I said.'Let's have a look, I'll soon get it out.'

But it was stuck in fast. Right through past the barb. No chance.

'Well,' I said, with an air of 'You brought it on yourself' (bit of a cheek, I know, but it worked), 'we'll have to get you down to the hospital.'

I led Sid to the car, moaning and holding his earole. Every now and then willing myself to NOT see the funny side of it. Things are always funnier when you know you mustn't laugh, ain't they? Roy never saw nothing funny in it, though. He had a fixed, wide-eyed and worried look all the way through the episode.

At the hospital, they sorted him out. From the receptionist to the nurses to the doctor who finally disgorged Sid, they all laughed their bollocks off. It was such a relief. Even Sid managed a smile.

I told you I caught a BIG 'UN, didn't I?

Like I said, if we saw a 'Private Fishing' sign, we homed in. They didn't put up those signs for a laugh. Here was a stretch of water teaming with bored fish just waiting to have a go at someone's maggot. But fishing in these places had its drawbacks as well. Fishing is supposed to be a relaxing pastime, but we had to be on the alert all the while. We done a 'runner' on many occasions. Not that I was particularly bothered about that side of it personally. I quite enjoyed it really. There was something exciting about being chased across the fields, hearing 'Oi! You!' behind you in the distance. It took me back to my scrumpin' days. Nevertheless I think I was on my own in this respect. Roy was a bit older than me an' got puffed out easier. He devised a plan that would mean if we got caught, we wouldn't have to run.

'It's simple,' Roy said. 'What we do is, if we get caught, we pretend we're foreigners and don't understand a word their saying. They'll get fed up trying to get through to us and just tell us to bugger off.'

'Roy, you're a genius! We'll be Germans.' We'd been to Germany. 'We can convince 'em with a couple of 'Jas' and 'Neins', and we'll be able to move off peacefully.' So this was the plan.

A 'Private Fishing' sign was spotted and we were there. This time Sid wasn't with us. He'd traded his fishing tackle in for a set of golf clubs. (Gawd help Mick, Moss and Cliff!) Tony Dudley, the new trumpet player in the band, decided to come along with me and Roy. Tony at the time was into neither fishing nor golf, but the basic fishing equipment (a stick and a bit of string) was cheaper than a set of golf clubs, so Tony came fishing.

We'd been fishing for about an hour, me and Roy with proper rods and reels and Tony with his stick and a bit of string, when we spied these two geezers walking towards us along the bank. You could tell by their faces they meant business.

'Don't forget we're Germans,' said Roy, looking down the bank at the geezers, with a big daft foreigner's grin on his face.

'Guten Tag,' said Roy, as they approached, still grinning like a nutter. 'Oh, no, he's overdone it,' I thought. But no, they hadn't sussed. They hadn't quite caught what Roy had said, but they sensed we weren't locals. At this point they probably figured we were from the next county.

'Guten Tag,' Roy said again, showing all his teeth. He had a lot of teeth too.

'Look mate,' said one of the blokes, 'this is private fishing here and you're coming with us to the police station.'

'Ja?' said Roy, still grinning. I thought he was overdoing it but it convinced 'em.

'They're fuckin' foreigners,' said the other bloke. 'Cheeky bastards.'

I realised then that although Roy was right in the fact that we could convince them we were foreigners, he was wrong in the idea that we were going to get off light. It was obvious that they didn't like 'fuckin' foreigners' who 'come over here and think they can do as they fuckin' well like'. 'Look,' said the first bloke to Roy. 'You (pointing at Roy) are *fishing* (making casting-out movements) in PRIVATE (doing some other movement) WATERS' (pointing at the river). He looked at his mate, satisfied with himself.

'You,' he said again, pointing at Roy, 'must give me your rod. I take it away 'cos you break the law' (making 'gimme-that-here' movements towards Roy's rod).

'Oh yah, yah!' Roy's away. 'Mein rodden ist gut! Glassen fieber! Eine guten Deutsche rodden. Danke Shoen! Eine Hundert pounds,' said Roy, offering it to the bloke but keeping a tight grip on it.

'Oh for fuck sake', said the geezer to his mate. 'He thinks I want to buy the fuckin' thing.' Up 'til now, me and Tone have kept a low profile. There wasn't much point in joining in, Roy seemed to be doing alright. But they weren't getting through to Roy. I should have been ready for it, but I wasn't.

'Do you speak English?' they said to Tony. Tony shit himself.

'Owgli mumpa shlafen,' was all he could muster up.

It didn't mean fuck all but they were none the wiser. I was watching Tony, wondering what noises he was going to come up with next when they turned to me. I was taken by surprise.

'What about you. Do you speak any English at all?'

I put myself right in it. 'A leetle,' I said, making a finger-and-thumb movement. What a stupid idiot! *I* was now the bloke to talk to.

'Thank Christ for that,' they said and he began to explain the Private Fishing bit and the rod confiscation bit all over again to me. I had to nod in a knowing way and try to explain to Roy what he was on about. It wasn't easy with Roy grinnin' at me like a nutter. Tony hid behind a tree. I knew he was quietly having hysterics. This didn't help matters. I had enough to contend with. What with Roy's nutter face, which he nodded every now and then, I really had to think of horrible things in case I laughed and ruined everything.

Roy did help me out in the end. When he felt like I'd got to the punchline of all the bollocks I'd been rattling off as an explanation, he took on a concerned look. For the first time he closed his mouth and hid his teeth. He *did* look concerned. He began making apologies in German of course but they seemed to suss what he was on about. They weren't particularly impressed, but by now they were getting fed up with the whole thing.

'Go on, bugger off,' they said, resigning themselves to the fact they weren't getting anywhere.

Thank Christ for that, I thought. It's over. We don't do THAT again!

Now there's an old saying that all's well that ends well. But for us it hadn't ended. Let alone *well!* We all three made our way to the car. Not daring to look at or speak to each other. We each knew what the others were thinking. As soon as we were in the car and on our way, *are we gonna have a good laugh or WHAT!*

'Quick, gimme the key,' said Roy, quietly.

'I haven't got the key,' I said.

'Yes, you have,' said Roy. 'You got the rods out of the boot.'

'Oh yeh, you're right, they're in the boot,' I said.

'What!'

'They're in the boot,' I repeated, wondering what the raised voice was all about. All he had to do was turn the knob that opens the boot and get 'em out. Let's go!

But no. Roy had a new Ford Cortina. The boot worked in a different way to my old 1100. The key opened the boot, but the boot locked automatically when you shut the lid down.

Worse was to come. Not only had I locked the key in the boot, that was bad enough, but the two bailiff geezers were waiting in their car for us to get out of the way. We were blocking their path.

'What do we do now?'

'You'll have to go and tell 'em what's happened,' said Roy.

'Hold up a minute. How do I explain this? I'm supposed to be German. I can't talk English.'

'You told 'em you speak a "leetle".'

'Yer, but I don't *wanna* talk to 'em anymore. Why can't Tony go?'

'Chas, don't be daft.' I knew he was right. There was no way out. The two geezers were looking more and more impatient by the minute. I went over to their car and explained what happened. I must have done it alright. They didn't suss.

'Okay,' they said (muttering 'fucking foreigners' under their breath). 'Come with us to the police station and we'll get you another key.'

I froze. I realised in an instant what would happen. There's bound to be some cocky copper there who speaks German and I'm fucked. Roy, in fact, could speak quite good German. He'd spent more time than us in Hamburg. Roy was the one who should go with them. At least he can get away with it if someone starts spouting off in German. Roy's going whether he likes it or not. Anyway, it was *his* idea to be Germans.

I explained in the best way I could that instead of me, my friend will go with them to the station.

'No, we want *you* to come. He can't speak English.'

Oh Christ! 'Eine moment,' I said. I wanted to jump into the river, but I walked back to the car. Roy had now developed, once more, his irritating daft foreigner's grin.

'Roy,' I said, between my teeth, 'you've got to go with 'em to get a key. They want me to go, but I'm not gonna risk it. I don't care what they say, I don't care if I have to own up, but I'm not going with them to the police station. If I have to talk German to a copper, I'm gonna blow it. You can speak German. There's bound to be a copper there who speaks it a bit. I'll be sussed out in no time. I *refuse to go.*'

'Alright, alright,' said Roy, 'I'll go.'

Off he's gone. I see his head nodding and his hands waving about as he's

Hurry up and take the picture before we get caught!

talking to 'em. I see their heads shaking and waving their hands about as they're trying to answer. In the end they all nod and Roy gets in, looking round at us. He still had his fixed foreign nutter's grin but it didn't seem so irritating this time.

They arrived back an hour later. No luck with the key. Roy had an entertaining time, though. He didn't meet up with any German-speaking copper, but he enjoyed himself listening to what they were saying about him. 'German bastard!' 'What are we helping him for?' 'Fuckin' well go back where they come from.' 'Coming over here thinking they can do as they like!'

We ended up ripping the lining out of the inside of the car to get to the boot. The next time we got caught fishing in 'Private' territory, we took the easy way out.

We run.

Chapter 15
Cliff and The Rebs Split

Roy Young, who fronted The Rebel Rousers when Cliff wasn't singing, had a great Rock 'n' Roll voice. Many people preferred him to Cliff. In fact, for out-and-out Little Richard-type Rock 'n' Roll, Roy was better, but he wasn't quite as versatile as Cliff. Cliff had the 'Soul' thing together, and kept the band in shape. I sang a bit, but reluctantly at the time.

Around the beginning of 1968 (I can't remember how it came about, I think we just wanted a change), The Rebel Rousers split from Cliff Bennett to go on their own. In theory, the idea was good. It could have worked. Trouble was, none of us had any real business sense. We thought we'd go straight back on the road earning almost as much money as we did with Cliff. I knew the band was still good and thought that would be enough, but promoters weren't as enthusiastic about booking us without Cliff. The gigs dwindled and so did the money.

Sid got fed up being skint and went back to his old job as a typewriter mechanic. The rest of us, me, Roy, Mick, Moss and John Golden (the new trumpet player who replaced Tony Dudley towards the end of Cliff Bennett) knew we had to get some work quick. We got offered a couple of weeks work in a club in Munich. The money wasn't good but it was better than nothing. Harvey Hinsley, my old guitar-playing mate from The Outlaws, came with us too. He'd come to see us on a gig just before we went and we wanted a guitar player. The prospects weren't exactly fantastic, and Harvey had now settled in a 'proper' job, which he went back to when The Outlaws split up. But Harvey fancied the idea. He threw his job in and was on the road again. Germany! We had a gig!

We arrived at the PN Club, Munich, tired but eager and ready to go. We found out that we had to play for about five hours a night. Great! Perfect for whipping the band into shape. There was a small obstacle to overcome, though. We only had two hours of material. 'Well, we'll have to do 'Special Requests' for songs we've done earlier, plus double or triple solos for everyone in each song, and don't forget Burty's drum solos are quite long. You can even make them a bit longer, Mick. Throw everything in.' He did.

Mick played his solo, tapped all up and down the mike stands with his sticks, got up from his drums, tapped all round the stage, all round the club, on people's beer glasses, people's heads, back on the stage, stood one-legged on his tom-tom while still playing it and finished off telling a joke on the mike. It killed a lot of time. But not enough.

It was the first night. After a couple of sets, we worked out we were still gonna be short. Something had to be done. But what? Half-way through the night I was stuck. We'd done all the requests, except – it suddenly came to me!

'Ladies and Gentlemen,' I said. ' We have a special request for Mick Burt to do his solo again. 'WAY YOU GO, MICK!'

Mick looked at me daggers, but he was a trooper. Off he went. Boomp . . . boomp . . . boomp, all round the stage, all round the club, back on the stage, did the one-legged bit on his tom-tom and told a joke (the same one). He went down a storm! Mick cheered up a bit. We were in shape so far and winning. We only had one more 45-minute set to go.

We got through the first half hour somehow. Just 15 more minutes. But now we were well and truly stuck. We'd done requests three and four times, and three and four piano and brass solos in each. We've got to think of something. There was nothing else for it. 'Ladies and Gentlemen. In response to many requests, Mick Burt is going to do you another drum solo!'

'No, Charlie, I'm not,' said Mick, through his teeth.

'You've got to, Mick,' I said, trying hard not to let the crowd know what was happening. 'If we come off early, we might get knocked. We've done everything else three or four times. We've only done the drum solo *twice*. Do a short one.'

'Here he is, Ladies and Gentlemen, MICK BURT!'

Boomp . . . boomp . . . boomp . . . boomp . . . Off Mick's gone looking even less happy this time. But he *did* shorten it. He *didn't* tap all round the stage. He *didn't* tap all round the club. He *didn't* tell a joke. He never got that far. He only got as far as his one legged tom-tom bit.

I swear to this day, Mick, as far as I know, nobody tampered with your tom-tom. Mick was there, on one leg, on the tom-tom, playing it at the same time. One of the tom-tom legs collapsed and threw Mick into the crowd!

'You bastard, Charlie!' he shouted from the club floor. 'You wait 'til I fuckin' get hold of you. You fuckin' loosened that tom-tom leg!'

'Mick, I didn't. Honest!' I didn't either, honest! But because I laughed, he wouldn't have it.

He didn't really hurt himself, it was the shock really. He grazed his shin a bit, that was all, but he wouldn't have it that I didn't do it on purpose. I have been known to play tricks, but I wouldn't do one that would hurt anybody. It was funny though, Mick. And you did get us through to the end of the night!

We started rehearsing in the daytime to get a few new numbers off. The band got better, but it was never very disciplined. Perhaps it was the years spent before under the iron hand of Cliff Bennett, with fines for drunkenness and all that. The New Rebel Rousers had no such rules. The last set was always a free-for-all. By that time, a few pints of German lager had been sunk. Moss and John would decide that 'Gambols' (Moss's word) was a good idea. 'Gambols' was Moss and John running up and down the club floor doing somersaults, and John, every now and again, chucking his trumpet to Moss, and Moss missing it most of the time. John's trumpet ended up looking like a little brass concertina. How he still managed to play it, I don't know, but he did.

One night, after doing our first couple of sets, we were told that there was a couple of geezers in the club that wanted to buy us a drink and have a chat to us. We all went over and it turned out they wanted to book us toplay in Vienna. They were starting a club there and wanted us to open it. (They caught us at the right time. The first couple of sets were usually pretty good and we were reasonably sober.) We talked money and it was good. Much better than we were getting in Munich. The deal was done on the spot. We were to open their club about a month later, and were to play there for three weeks. Great! We shook hands on the deal and carried on talking socially.

I did notice that the two blokes kept calling Roy 'Cleef' all the time, but just passed it off as getting names mixed up. As people often do.

They got onto the subject of our past visits to Germany. The Beatles tour and that. 'Cleef Bennett and The Rebel Rousers for a long time have a good name in Germany. We notice you have not done 'Got To Get You Into My Life' yet. Will you do it, Cleef, when you go back for your next set?' Suddenly it dawned on me, and Roy at the same time. It wasn't just a simple case of getting names mixed up. They thought Roy was Cliff Bennett! I was just about to speak when Roy gave me a look of 'For fuck sake don't say nothing'. I didn't. I left it to him. He mumbled something about . . . 'haven't done it for a long time' and we went off to do our next set. At long last, we finished the set. I was dying to find out what the next move was gonna be. We met over the road at the pub.

'Roy,' I said. 'What the fuck we gonna do? We've *got* to tell him!'

'We'll worry about that later,' said Roy. 'We can't tell him now, we'll blow the whole thing. We need the money. Once we're there, even if hedoes find out, it'll be too late for him to find another band. He likes what we're doing anyway. He won't be able to find a band good enough to replace us. We can laugh it off as a misunderstanding, but we'll be *there*! Earning the money.'

'Roy! Once he finds out it's not Cliff Bennett and The Rebel Rousers, he won't want to know. All the punters will be asking for their money back. Let's laugh it off as a misunderstanding *now* and take a chance.'

I was still slightly in two minds, and if Roy had come upwith an answer to this, I would have gone along with it. We all needed the money but we decided to come clean. We went and sat with them after the next set.

'Chas seems to think that you think I'm Cliff Bennett,' said Roy, trying to smile casually through a face that I could see was full of panic. We waited for the answer. Our immediate future rested upon it.

'You are not Cliff Bennett? I must say, I thought you were.' (Here it comes.) 'No matter. You are better without him.'

We all laughed. A bit too heartily for what the remark called for. But the Austrian was pleased with himself. He liked our sense of humour, and he was looking forward to seeing us in Vienna in a month's time. 'So long, Cleef,' he said at the end of our talk. We all laughed again.

As I said, the money was good, better than Munich anyway. We decided we could afford to bring our wives and kids over with us. They hadn't had much of a time, not much money and all that. It could be a bit of a working holiday for all of us. Roy was in touch with Lippy (the main Austrian who run the club) in the few weeks that preceded the gig, sorting out hotel arrangements, arrival times, etc. Roy suggested to me that, rather than stay in a hotel, why don't he get Lippy to fix up a flat for me and him and our wives and kids. Somewhere we could cook for ourselves if we wanted to. It would save a lot ofmoney. Good idea! Roy fixed it up with Lippy.

I was looking forward to it. So was Joan. Juliet was about a year old at the time. We all went in our own cars. I kept my fingers crossed my old 1100 would make it. It did. We arrived about midnight on the night before we were due to play. Me and Joan were dog-tired and ready for bed. Juliet, like kids are, was wide-awake and ready for action. But then she'd been cooped up in the back of the motor for hundreds of miles.

'Let's get to the flat quick,' I said to Joan. 'And we can let her loose to crawl about all she wants. When she's had enough, we can put her to bed and we can just flop into ours.'

We found the club and I went to find Lippy. Roy was there, all smiles. He'd arrived about an hour earlier. He was with Lippy.

'Good to see you, Chas,' said Lippy.

'Lippy's gonna show us where the flat is,' said Roy.

'Follow me,' says Lippy. Out into the street we've gone and followed Lippy's car all round the back streets of Vienna. We finally come to a stop in some little street. 'There's the flat,' said Lippy, pointing to a dingy doorway, 'and here's the key. Sleep well. I look forward to seeing you tomorrow.'

I didn't take too much notice of the look of the outside. I didn't expect a mansion. Roy opened the door and went in. The passageway was a bit dismal, but nobody said nothing, we were too tired.

We woke up when we saw the actual flat itself, though! Talk about a khasi! My Nan's coal cupboard back at 11, Harton Road was cleaner!

'Fuckin' hell!' said Roy quietly. I don't think I said anything. I just looked.

'Fuckin' hell!' said Roy again, a bit louder. I still don't think I said anything. I was trying to will myself into thinking it wasn't too bad. I was knackered.

'Fuckin' hell!' said Roy, loud and positive. 'We ain't staying here.'

I knew he was right. We'll all end up with the plague.

'I'm getting on the phone to Lippy,' said Roy, and so he did.

Lippy came down and looked concerned. He knew full well what it was like all the time, crafty bastard. 'I am sorry. I was assured it was a clean flat.'

'Clean flat!!!' Juliet escaped our clutches once or twice and crawled about the floor. She had a snow-white Babygro on when we arrived. Now she looked like she'd been up the chimney.

'I fix you up another flat tomorrow.'

'Fair enough, but what about tonight?' said Roy.

'Okay, I find you a hotel.'

A hotel was found, and Lippy promised to sort us out a flat as soon as possible.

When the news got back to the band, certain members (who shall remain nameless until about two paragraphs' time) interpreted this episode as 'special treatment' from the promoter. 'Unfair! Staying in a posh hotel while we stay in an ordinary one.'

A couple of days later, me and Roy and our families were still staying at the hotel. Lippy hadn't managed to find us a flat yet. On the third day, Lippy found us a flat. He also fixed up a gig on the same day, supporting Bill Haley at the big concert hall in town. The plan was to rehearse for the concert in the afternoon.

By the time me and Roy had checked out the flat and moved our families in, we'd gone well over the call-time for rehearsal. In our absence all this unrest in the band about me and Roy getting 'special treatment' (they were convinced *Roy* was at the bottom of it!) had come to a head.

Mick and Moss, fed up with waiting, decided to go to the local bar and air their grievances over a bottle of whisky. By the time me and Roy arrived, three hours later, Mick and Moss were back in the dressing-room, hardly able to stand and were MAD! They had *decided* Roy was well in with the promoter and had taken Charlie along with him for credibility. Staying in Posh Hotels, probably getting free dinners as well. SPECIAL TREATMENT! Who the fuck does he think he is? At that moment me and Roy walked into the dressing-room. 'Sorry about being late,' said Roy, genuinely, but unfortunately he sometimes had a way of making himself look really 'showbizzy' patronising. Mick became a wild man. 'Sorry about being late! We've been stuck here three hours waiting for you while you've been enjoying yourself having free dinners and everything else!'

'Mick, take it easy man.'

That done it. 'Take it easy man?' said Mick, 'I'll show you how to take it easy. Cunty!'

With that, Mick's gone at Roy with a snare drum stand. He was gonna hit him on the head with it, and he meant it. Crash! The drum stand misses Roy's head and embeds itself in the dressing-room door. Mick's gone for Roy. Roy's dodged him. I've grabbed Mick. 'What's the matter, calm down, Mick!'

'I'll fuckin' have you, cunty!' Mick's WILD!

'It's not you, Charlie, it's him! I know what he's fuckin' like. You bastard, Youngy, I'll fuckin' have you! Crawlin' round the promoter's arse, havin' free dinners and that. CUNTY!!!'

'Mick,' I said, holding him back with all my strength. At that moment, Lippy's slung his head in the door.

'Boys! You're on *now*!' Duty called. All was forgotten for the minute. The magic words had been said. 'You're on.' And out we went. To perform the worst show we'd ever done in our lives.

Lippy had arranged, as a 'show stopper', for Moss and John to chop up a grand piano halfway through the act. Halfway through the act? Wewere lucky to get through the first tune. Burty played like the wild man hewas. Keith Moon wasn't in his class. It might have been good, but it was fuck-all to do with what *we* were doing. Then the two axes were passed to Moss and John, to do their bit on the grand piano.

It was a real grand piano. Shame really. It was a better one than we had. Moss and John laid into it. Two wild men, both pissed. They managed to wreck the piano, narrowly escaping chopping each other's knee caps. Moss, now drunk with power too, decides to finish off with a duck walk along the edge of the stage, blowing a sax solo at the same time.

A good idea in theory, but in Moss's state his sense of balance wasn't quite up to par. He teetered a couple of times but managed to right himself. It was a high stage, about 10 feet. Quite pretty too. It was surrounded by ferns and little trees in pots. Bracing himself for his final blast he let go with a high pitched 'WHEEEEEEEE', teetered, and almost like it was part of the act, disappeared off the edge of the stage. The ferns parted and came together. Then they were still. I watched the ferns. As I walked to the edge of the stage, the ferns started moving again.

They began to wobble and a couple fell over. Thank God. Something was happening down there. Two little hands appeared over the edge ofthe stage, then a face, with a stupid grin on it. The next minute Moss, helped by other willing hands from the front row, was back on stage in a heap.

He wasn't gonna be beat, though. He was up on his feet ready to finish the round. He grabbed his sax, closed his eyes and went for it. He was gonna finish his solo in style. Only he couldn't get his mouth round the mouthpiece. No wonder. You see, the sax broke his fall. The mouthpiece was the bit that hit the floor first. It was now bent round in a U shape, instead of being stuck out in the usual way at right-angles. Moss opened his eyes, studied his sax for a bit, figured out that the only way he could get at it was to turn the sax upside down, did so, closed his eyes again and away he went. It was a sight to see.

We got a write-up next day in one of the Austrian papers. I don't know what it said. We were told, 'It is best you do not get this write-up translated into English.'

After the Bill Haley concert, we had to go back to the club. We had another show to do and Moss wasn't finished yet.

Mick's drum solo had now become a featured part of the act. It was particularly liked by a bunch of geezers who came to the club every night. They were sort of well-to-do hard nuts and were well respected by the club owner (I got the impression that their line of business wasn't the type of thing you'd find advertised in the yellow pages). They showed their appreciation of the songs they liked by chucking screwed-up bank notes onto the stage. Burty's drum solo attracted them notes like a magnet. The more he banged the more them notes flew up. He was like a man possessed! That night the inevitable drum solo was requested by 'The Boys'. 'Bang' and 'Zip'. A note flew up and landed on his snare drum, 'WALLOP!' went Mick and two more bounced off his tom-tom. 'BOOM-BOOM-BOOM-BOOM-BOOM-BOOM!' Mick went mad. Notes flying all over the place. No more did he moan about doing a solo. In fact he was a bit choked that we now had a reasonable repertoire which meant he only had to do one solo a night.

Then, 'BOOM . . . BOOM . . . B-B-B-B-B-B-BOOM!!' Mick played a pattern that sounded like it was our cue to come back in. I realised by the look on Mick's face that he hadn't meant to do it. So did everybody else.

Except Moss.

No amount of arm waving and shaking of heads was gonna convince him. He'd heard the cue and that was it. Everybody else was wrong as far as he was concerned. He leapt in for his final 'Toot-toot-toot-ta-ta-toot-toot-toot'. But he never got as far as the first 'Toot'.

He had that Rock 'n' Roll sax player's style of leaning back when he went for a note. It worked well when he was sober. But he wasn't. He leant back raising the sax to his lips. But the sax never reached his lips. He just kept leaning back.

One minute Burty was looking at the back of Moss's head. The next minute he was looking at Moss's face, at his feet, upside down, still trying to 'Toot'. Moss had fallen backwards into the drum kit, the drums scattering in all directions like they'd been blown up. Burty stood up and bowed drunkenly to his fans. Needless to say, the number ended there, the rest of us trying to play some sort of Rock 'n' Roll fanfare as if the whole thing was planned. Screwed-up notes began to shower the stage!

A couple of the well-to-do hard nuts rushed the stage and hoisted Burty bodily over the débris and plonked him down onto their table. They poured him drinks and patted him on the back and stuffed screwed-up notes down his shirt. They thought it was a tremendous finish. We left Mick among the hoods, grinning from ear to ear, while we escorted Moss back to his hotel. I didn't envy the aches he was gonna wake up with in the morning. From the head downwards.

Apart from the 'odd occasions' which I've just mentioned, the Viennese gig was successful. The club owner was well pleased with the band (!) and we left for home with a few bob in our pockets.

The next gig we got offered was six weeks in Beirut.

Beirut, at that time, had more clubs in one square mile than anywhere else in the world. I enjoyed it there. It was the first time that I felt like I was in a *real* foreign country. Things like pomegranates growing (my favourite fruit) and locust beans which I lived on when I was a kid (my own kids don't like 'em, though; I bought some a while ago and they said they made 'em sick).

Also it was the feeling that Jesus in his day used to swan about round there. I am a fan of Jesus. Don't get me wrong that I mention Him so lightly, I mean it. He probably ate locust beans and pomegranates. I wonder if he swallowed the pips or spit them out? Some people do and some people don't. I always spit them out. My mum said you get consumption through swallowing pomegranate pips.

I visited Sidon while I was there. That was where Jesus performed one of His miracles. A woman came up to Him and said her son was ill. 'Go home and he'll be alright,' He said. And he was.

I went to Byblos too. The word 'Bible' comes from the name of the city. I know quite a bit about the Bible. More than Dave anyway. When Dave says he was 'well pleased' and I tell him that the Lord said that in the Bible about Jesus, 'My son in whom I am well pleased' – he thinks I'm having him on. But it's true. I often get the old Gideon's Bible out and have a read when we're staying in hotels.

The club was a typical sort of disco effort that you'd find anywhere in the world. It was called 'La Locomotive', and we were to open it. Perhaps our reputation for 'opening' clubs got round.

It was a bit weird at first. Although night clubs are basically the same wherever you go in the world (they're all based on American clubs), the punters are always different. At least they look different. They always act the same once they know what they are supposed to be doing. But a club full ofArabs, most of them with their headdresses on, seemed to present a bit of a challenge from the off. What do we do? Arabic music always seemed to me to sound like western music played backwards. But after a couple of nights I realised I was thinking too ethnic. All they wanted was western style 'Git-up-and-down-with-it' disco beat funk. Just like everywhere else. And they danced just as bad.

The disc jockey, George (couldn't have been his real name), done his best to guide us. 'I naw vot zer pipple vont. You do ze slow vun so zey ken grop itch udder and zen zer fonky fing.' Alright, George. We did our normal set and they liked us. Why not? It was good and we now kept reasonably sober. Roughly towards the middle of the night, we did that we always done, the 'Rock 'n' Roll Show'. It was my favourite part of the night. Roy Young did his Fats Domino and Little Richard bit and I did my Jerry Lee bit.

BRITAIN'S TOP 50

record retailer and music industry news

Pos	Title	Artist	Last three weeks	Label
1	ALL OR NOTHING	Small Faces	(2) (3) (9)	Decca F 12470
2	DISTANT DRUMS	Jim Reeves	(6) (17) (22)	RCA Victor RCA 1537
3	YELLOW SUBMARINE/ ELEANOR RIGBY	Beatles	(1) (1) (1)	Parlophone R 5493
4	TOO SOON TO KNOW	Roy Orbison	(5) (8) (17)	London HLU 10067
5	GOD ONLY KNOWS	Beach Boys	(3) (2) (2)	Capitol CL 15459
6	GOT TO GET YOU INTO MY LIFE	Cliff Bennett	(15) (18) (23)	Parlophone R 5489
7	THEY'RE COMING TO TAKE ME AWAY HA-HAA!	Napoleon XIV	(4) (4) (4)	Warner Bros. WB 5831
8	WORKING IN THE COAL MINE	Lee Dorsey	(10) (19) (29)	Stateside SS 528
9	LOVERS OF THE WORLD UNITE	David and Jonathan	(7) (9) (10)	Columbia DB 7950
10	JUST LIKE A WOMAN	Manfred Mann	(11) (13) (16)	Fontana TF 730
11	MAMA	Dave Berry	(8) (6) (5)	Decca F 12435
12	LITTLE MAN	Sonny & Cher	(35) (—) (—)	Atlantic 584-040
13	YOU CAN'T HURRY LOVE	Supremes	(38) (—) (—)	Tamla-Motown TMG 575
14	I'M A BOY	Who	(20) (42) (—)	Reaction 591-004
15	WHEN I COME HOME	Spencer Davis Group	(23) (38) (—)	Fontana TF 739
16	ASHES TO ASHES	Mindbenders	(22) (29) (45)	Fontana TF 731
17	I SAW HER AGAIN	Mama's and Papa's	(13) (11) (13)	RCA Victor RCA 1533
18	MORE THAN LOVE	Ken Dodd	(16) (15) (14)	Columbia DB 7976
19	VISIONS	Cliff Richard	(12) (7) (7)	Columbia DB 7968
20	HI-LILI HI-LO	Alan Price Set	(14) (12) (11)	Decca F 12442
21	WITH A GIRL LIKE YOU	Troggs	(9) (5) (3)	Fontana TF 717
22	HOW SWEET IT IS	Junior Walker	(27) (32) (43)	Tamla-Motown TMG 571
23	WALK WITH ME	Seekers	(31) (—) (—)	Columbia DB 8000
24	THE MORE I SEE YOU	Chris Montez	(18) (14) (8)	Pye 7N 25369
25	LAND OF 1000 DANCES	Wilson Pickett	(34) (41) (—)	Atlantic 584-039
26	WINCHESTER CATHEDRAL	New Vaudeville Band	(42) (—) (—)	Fontana TF 741
27	BLACK IS BLACK	Los Bravos	(19) (16) (6)	Decca F 22419
28	SUMMER IN THE CITY	Lovin' Spoonful	(17) (10) (12)	Kama-Sutra KAS 200
29	BIG TIME OPERATOR	Zoot Money	(28) (25) (32)	Columbia DB 7975
30	I CAN'T TURN YOU LOOSE	Otis Redding	(32) (33) (42)	Atlantic 584-030
31	LOVING YOU IS SWEETER THAN EVER	Four Tops	(21) (22) (26)	Tamla-Motown TMG 568
32	SUNNY	Bobby Hebb	(45) (—) (—)	Philips BF 1503
33	RUN	Sandie Shaw	(43) (—) (—)	Pye 7N 17163
34	AIN'T TOO PROUD TO BEG	Temptations	(25) (21) (24)	Tamla-Motown TMG 565
35	BAREFOOTIN'	Robert Parker	(24) (24) (25)	Island WI 286
36	BLOWIN' IN THE WIND	Stevie Wonder	(37) (37) (38)	Tamla-Motown TMG 570
37	BEND IT!	Dave Dee, Dozy, Beaky, Mick & Tich	(—) (—) (—)	Fontana TF 746
38	STRANGERS IN THE NIGHT	Frank Sinatra	(29) (26) (27)	Reprise R 23052
39	SUMMERTIME	Billy Stewart	(46) (—) (—)	Chess CRS 8040
40	I DON'T CARE	Los Bravos	(44) (—) (—)	Decca F 22484
41	ALL I SEE IS YOU	Dusty Springfield	(—) (—) (—)	Philips BF 1510
42	WARM AND TENDER LOVE	Percy Sledge	(39) (34) (34)	Atlantic 584-034
43	GUANTANAMERA	Sandpipers	(—) (—) (—)	Pye 7N 25380
44	I WANT YOU	Bob Dylan	(26) (20) (18)	CBS 202258
45	STOP THAT GIRL	Chris Andrews	(36) (36) (47)	Decca F 22472
46	GIVE ME YOUR WORD	Billy Fury	(33) (27) (30)	Decca F 12459
47	BORN A WOMAN	Sandy Posey	(—) (—) (—)	MGM MGM 1321
48	OUT OF TIME	Chris Farlowe	(30) (23) (15)	Immediate IM 035
49	CHANGES	Crispian St. Peters	(—) (—) (—)	Decca F 12480
50	SOMEWHERE MY LOVE	Mike Sammes Singers	(—) (—) (—)	HMV POP 1546

(Numbers in brackets indicate last three week's positions)

Ain't too proud to beg. Belinda 34
All I see is you. Belinda 41
All or nothing. Robbins 1
Ashes to ashes. Screen Gems 16
Barefootin'. Island 35
Bend it! Lynn 37
Big time operator. Bermanta Music 29
Black is black. Robert Mellin 27
Blowin' in the wind. Blossom 36
Born a woman. Painted Desert Music 47
Changes. Essex 49
Distant drums. Acuff Rose 2
Give me your word. Connelly 46
God only knows. Immediate 5
Got to get you into my life. Northern 6
Guantanamera. Harmony 43
Hi-lili Hi-lo. Robbins 20
How sweet it is. Belinda 22
I can't turn you loose. Copy Control 30
I don't care. Palace 40
I'm a boy. Fabulous 14
I saw her again. Dick James 17
I want you. Feldman 44
Land of 1,000 dances. Dick James 25
Little man. Belinda 12
Lovers of the world unite. Mills 9
Loving you is sweeter than ever. Jobete MI 31
Mama. Francis Day and Hunter 11
More than love. Keith Prowse 18
Out of time. Mirage 48
Run. Glissando 33
Somewhere my love. Robbins 50
Stop that girl. Glissando 45
Strangers in the night. Welbeck 38
Summer in the city. Faithful Virtue BMI 28
Summertime. Chappell 39
Sunny. Campbell Connelly 32
The more I see you. Bregman 24
They're coming to take me away. Copyright 7
Too soon to know. Acuff Rose 4
Visions. Joaneline-Belinda 19
Walk with me. Springfield 23
Warm and tender love. Belinda 42
When I come home. Island 15
Winchester Cathedral. Meteor 26
With a girl like you. Dick James 21
Working in the coal mine. Ardmore and Beechwood 8
Yellow submarine/Eleanor Rigby. Northern Songs 3
You can't hurry love. Belinda 13

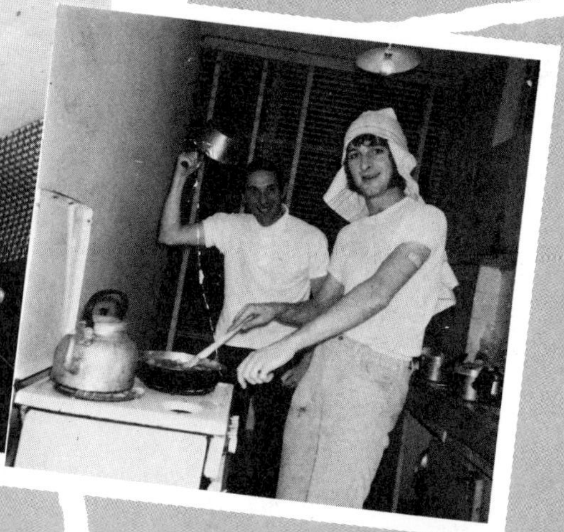

Top Me with Cliff on bass. Reading University, 1967. **Left** Sid, Cliff and me at Burtons, Uxbridge on New Year's Eve, 1965. **Right** Burty and me in Beirut, 1969. He tried to push me through that window behind once. He didn't mean it tho'.

We did it well.

But the punters didn't like it, said George.

My back was up. Stupid bastards don't know what they're listening to. This was Rock 'n' Roll! Played from the heart! George'd say, 'Do not play ze Rack 'n' Rolly. Play ze funky fing. Zer pipple do not understand. Zay nat know zer rack music.'

It dawned on me that it was strange to them because they had never *heard* it before. It never reached Beirut in the Fifties. Well ain't it about time it did, then?

We persevered under pressure. The Rock 'n' Roll got better for it. It became an obsession with me. I was sure it would get through in the end 'cos it sounded so good.

I remember upsetting Harvey one night. After the end of the show he came up to me and said, 'I think we ought to cut out the Rock 'n' Roll bit.'

'Why?' I said. I knew he enjoyed it.

'My girl don't like it.' he said.

'Fuckin' hell! You wanna stop playing Rock 'n' Roll just 'cos some stupid bird don't reckon it? Bollocks!' P'raps I did upset him and it might have been an insult to his bird, but to me giving up Rock 'n' Roll was like putting your Dad in a home.

It won in the end.

The Little Richard bit, the Jerry Lee bit, the Fats Domino bit. People began asking specially for it. Even George. 'Do zer Rack 'n' Rolly. Zer pipple love it!'

By the time we left, it was the most requested part of the act.

Rock 'n' Roll Will Never Die!

We left for home just before Christmas with a welcome bit of bunce.

Them club gigs abroad paid alright really. Trouble was, the long gaps between used up any money we saved. We tried, in the best way weknew how, to get back into the recording scene, but nobody really wanted to know. We did manage to get one record out, 'Should I Or Shouldn't I?' It flopped and that was that.

Doing the clubs abroad was the only way we could be certain of making a few bob. We'd save as much as we could and hope the next gig come along quick. I had a good Christmas that year but by January I was skint again.

Chapter 16

Now What Can I Do To Get Some Money?

I did a few sessions and a few gigs here and there, but it wasn't enough. The Social Security were highly unsympathetic. The first and the last time I shall ever ask for their help. Me and Joan and Juliet were evicted from our flat. My old 1100 was nicked by the Bailiff – the scum of the Earth, who can only answer 'Somebody has to do it.'

Joan's Mum and Dad were great. They didn't have much room, but they took us in willingly. I think Joan's Mum had as much faith in me as Joan did. I was encouraged to stick at it. There was never so much as a mention of getting a 'proper' job. The worst of it was, I knew I was good at what I was doing but, at the time, I didn't know what to do *with* it. But, like I said earlier, all thoughts about doing your own thing go right out the window when you're skint. I felt guilty about being skint and all I could think about was where the next bit of *money* was coming from. The club thing seemed the only sure bet for *some* money. We just had to work on getting them more regular.

Me, Joan and Juliet were still living with Joan's Mum and Dad (Doris and Doug) and her brother Bruce when the next club gig came up. It was in the Bahamas.

Sounds great, don't it? But it ain't. It's a horrible place. Some people might like it, but I don't. It's too fuckin' hot.

I spent all my spare time with my head in the air-conditioning system in the flat. Mind you, we did go over in the height of summer. I've not been over in the winter. Perhaps it ain't so bad then. But the money was good – the main thing. We had a free flat, free drinks, and all we had to buy was our food, which we cooked ourselves, so it didn't work out too bad. But I was getting in a rut. Here we go again.

Earning alright, sure, but I was bored. Once again the punters only wanted music they could dance to. There's *got* to be a way of earning money by playing what I wanted to play, but I wasn't sure what I wanted to play yet. I knew it wasn't this. Playing music just so's people can dance, or wriggle about like cunts. The band began talking about, and doing, anything that wasn't to do with music. Football, fishing, these all began to sound more interesting than music. Something was wrong.

Music had always been my first love. I used to drop Dave Peacock a card now and again. I'd tell him all about some great Rock 'n' Roller or C & W artist I'd just seen on this new American TV programme, 'Hee Haw'. I was into music. This was all I wrote about to Dave. We had the same views on music. It was obvious that we should be making music together, but I never realised it then.

When we came back from the Bahamas, Roy left the band. He wanted to go out on his own. We got another singer for a while, Mike Stevens, but, although he wasn't a bad singer, the band's morale was sinking fast. What little spark was left, soon died. In the winter of 1969, The Rebel Rousers split up.

The short-lived Black Claw. Dave Peaco

ey Hinsley, Mick Burt and me.

I began doing a few more sessions with producer Derek Lawrence. I told him about Albert Lee. Albert became a regular. That suited me. I loved Albert's playing. He played *real* notes. Unlike many of the popular guitar heroes of the time. An Albert Lee album was got together, but was never released. We did another album with a black soul singer, Earl Jordan, featuring guitarists Ritchie Blackmore (who had now made a name for himself with Deep Purple), Jim Sullivan, and Albert Lee. The album was called 'Green Bullfrog'. Derek Lawrence had a thing about colours. He had a hit called 'White' something or other with some bird. That was it! Every record he put out after that had to have a colour in it. He suggested a number for me to record that this new American group, The Band, had out on an LP. They were good.

We recorded this song, 'Across the Great Divide'. I didn't think it was bad, but it wasn't as good as their version. It was recorded with session men but Derek wanted it to be put out under a band name. Jerry Reed had an instrumental out called 'The Claw'. I thought this would be a good name for a band. Del thought so too, but he had to get his colour into the name. After going through more colours that there are in the rainbow, we came to a compromise. I liked 'Black'. Derek argued that black wasn't really a colour, and as the whole point was that colours were lucky to him, we couldn't have it. When I pointed out that 'White' wasn't really a colour either, which was his original lucky colour. 'Black' suddenly became *the* colour. The only two colours that weren't colours – black and white! Why didn't he think of it before? 'Black Claw' became the name of the band, and the record was released.

It didn't do fuck all.

But a band called Black Claw was formed just the same, with the idea of making more records. The band members were: me (piano, doubling on guitar), Dave Peacock (bass), Mick Burt (drums) and Harvey Hinsley (guitar). We began doing gigs. Not many, but the ones we did went down well. The music we were making was good, and above all we were enjoying ourselves. Music was No 1 again. We accepted anything that was put our way. We just wanted to play.

We knew we had something, but it was gonna take a time toget it off the ground. We tried as best we could. We made an album for about £30 quid each. It was done in three hours. It wasn't a bad album either. It was called 'Country Pie'. We did it 'on the side' for another company. It's still around today. I've seen it on sale in Tesco's!

Harvey wasn't on that album. I overdubbed the guitar. Me, Dave and Mick. The line-up we have today. That was our first album. We had a disastrous trip to Berlin and a few more gigs here and there, but the band was short-lived. That old enemy, *poverty*, began to rear its ugly head once again.

I got a phone call from Albert Lee. He was joining a new group called 'Heads Hands and Feet'. They needed a bass player and he recommended me. I didn't want to leave the band 'cos I was happy, but I was skint. It was a hard decision to make, but all was agreed Black Claw's future looked dim without money behind us. And money was non-existent. Harvey got an offer to join Hot Chocolate, where he still is at the time of writing. Dave joined a C & W Band and Mick went back to his old job, plumbing.

In 1970, Heads Hands and Feet were formed.

Chapter 17
Heads Hands and Feet

The line-up was: me (bass), Albert Lee (guitar), Tony Colton (writer and lead vocalist), Ray 'Smiffy' Smith (writer and guitarist), Mike O'Neil (piano) and Pete Gavin (drums).

They were managed by Danny Secunda who had great hopes for the band. At about the same time, me and Joan got offered a council flat in Edmonton. It wasn't what we would have chosen for ourselves, but it was brand new and it was a place of our own. True it was a tower block and we were on the 22nd floor (frightening! I'm not mad on heights), but we, forever optimists, moved in and made the most of it.

That band had ambition. Not only to play good music. It also had plans to become world-famous. I'm not saying it couldn't have been. There were plenty of world-famous bands that were duff and we could play, so it didn't seem that unlikely. I wasn't so sure as I wanted to be famous with *this* band, though I realized then that you have to live with whatever makes you famous. I did like the band and most of the music, but not *all* of it.

Working with 'em taught me a lot though. It proved once and for all that no matter what talent you've got, you can't sit around hoping that people are going to recognise it. You've *got* to work at it. Talent plus hard work leads to success.

In 1970, guitar heroes were still very much in evidence amongst the 'world-famous' bands. But we had Albert Lee. My favourite English guitar player. My only reservation at the time was that perhaps he's too good, and most of the famous ones I didn't think were any good. Perhaps you had to be bad to be famous? No, that can't be right. There were one or two I liked. Albert can do it!

In England at the time Albert was known, or heard-of anyway. But the Trendies weren't particularly impressed. He wasn't loud enough, he wasn't distorted enough and never set light to his amp. On top of that, he liked Country and Western! I mean! The Trendies read the music papers and they always take the piss out of C & W. He can't be any good.

The music papers never took a lot of notice of Heads Hands and Feet. 'Old Albert? Yer, we know him. Plays all that cowboy music, don't he. Now ol' Nobby? Rotten bollocks, now THERE'S a GUITARIST for yer! Plays two notes at once! And farts in the pick-up to create a minor third. Fabulous! He makes the guitar sound like the Hallelujah Chorus.'

We went out to Los Angeles to do the Troubador shortly after we got together. We went down great. The Yanks saw the band for what they were – good.

They became interested in us in the States. We talked to Mort Lewis who wanted USA management. (He managed Simon and Garfunkel at the time.) The news filtered back to England. Suddenly the Press were interested. 'HEADS HANDS AND FEET GO DOWN WELL IN AMERICA.' 'ALBERT LEE IS ACCLAIMED AS A GREAT GUITARIST!' 'ANOTHER ONE OF OUR GREAT ENGLISH GUITARISTS KNOCKS THE YANKS FOR SIX!' 'SIMON AND

GARFUNKEL'S MANAGER LOVES THE BAND'. 'WE ALWAYS KNEW YOU'D MAKE IT ALBERT!' Or quotes to this effect, and the Trendies began to like Heads Hands and Feet. We *had* gone down well in America, and if I can generalise, the Americans use their *ears* more than the English. This is not being fair on the real English punters, but remember I'm generalising. A lot of music in England is judged with the *eyes*. Seems daft, don't it? But it's true. If they *read* something is good, then it is. If they read something's bad, then it is. In America they go by their ears. Music is important to them and is there to be listened to and not read about.

The Americans liked Albert's guitar playing. They knew he was good. But then their country was brought up on the guitar (and the gun). It's in the blood.

If the music you're making is good, whatever style, they'll like it, and they'll show it. Me, Dave and Mick went over to New York in 1980 amid cries from some people in England of 'Chas and Dave? You're too English. They won't understand you.' But they judge America from their front rooms. They haven't been there, playing to the people.

Chas and Dave went down great. They copped hold of the feeling of the music. The only thing that matters. The *way* we sang was fresh to them. You can tell when people come up to you after the gig. You can see it in their eyes if they're just being polite. If they really like you, they can't hide it. They liked Chas and Dave. 'Understand them? Why ask that question? We enjoyed it!' Why all this lark about understanding? Did the cave man understand it when he was having his first bunk-up? It didn't matter. He knew he was *enjoying* himself!

Heads Hands and Feet came back from America to a bit more receptive English audience. Our first album was well received in an underground sort of way, and we started doing the rounds of the Colleges and Universities. The first album was a double album titled Heads Hands and Feet. (It was released as a single album in England, a compilation of the two.) Our second album was called 'Tracks' and on June 19th, 1972 we went over to the States again for an eight-week tour. It was an experience. I loved it.

Just before we left, me and Joan moved from the tower block in Edmonton. We managed to get our own place. A little bungalow in Broxbourne. It was heaven. Me, Joan and Juliet and our new addition to the family, Katie.

The tour was pretty well organised. It all went smoothly considering we were jumping from tour to tour. We worked with people like Procul Harum, J. Geils, Humble Pie, Jethro Tull, Edgar Winter and others.

I'd watch 'em from the side of the stage. They were all good in their own way, but I had my favourites.

For sheer Rock 'n' Roll/Rhythm and Blues, it was J. Geils. For good tunes, Procul Harum. Excitement, Humble Pie (with Stevie Marriott). Jethro Tull put on a show and had a good sense of humour. Edgar Winter? Not my cup of tea really, but he did have something and I could see why he was liked.

We got about a bit, too, on that tour. Los Angeles, Alberquerque, Houston, Chicago, New York, St Louis, San Diego, Oklahoma, Denver.

I remember Denver!

We stayed at the Holiday Inn (where else?). We went through the normal routine on arrival. Check in, chuck the bags in the room and meet in the bar. I was first down. There at the bar, looking like they was really having a good time was the scruffiest, filthiest couple of characters you ever saw. At their feet was this little scruffy dog. They thought the world of it and with every round of drinks they would order it up a steak sandwich. I got talking to them and it turned out they were hillbillies. They'd come from the hills just outside Denver. I didn't ask questions as to how they come to be here, or, more to the point, how they didn't get thrown out. They were treated with respect by the staff. It was obvious to me, they must be a couple of gold prospectors and had struck it rich.

The rest of the boys came down and when the hillbillies found out we were musicians, they decided to throw a party that night. Drinks on them! Not only for us, but the whole of the hotel was invited. After the gig, we all met in this big room. The two hillbillies were the life and soul of the party. Someone somewhere had given one of 'em a Marguerita. (A murky sort of American cocktail, a ladies' drink really, the rim is dipped in salt and it's drunk out of a dinky glass.) They'd never seen anything like it before in their lives; but they were *gone* on it! 'Marguerita for everybody!' they shouted. 'And another steak sandwich!' (For the dog!) Me and Albert homed in on the grand piano and we Rock 'n' Rolled 'til the sun come up. Every now and then a couple more Margueritas arriving.

Next day, we all met by the swimming pool. There they were. Still drinking. Only now it was beer. (The salt in the Margueritas must have given 'em a thirst!) The old dog was now a-kip on a sun lounger. He was wet so he'd obviously been having a good swim around the pool. They livened up when they saw me.

'Hey Chas! You and Albert played great last night. What d'ya wanna drink?' Drink? How do these boys do it? 'I'll just have a coffee, if that's alright.'

'Sure, whatever you want. Hey, waiter. Bring our friend a coffee.'

'Hey, Luke!' he said to his mate. 'This little ol' piece of plastic can get us a plane ride!' He had in his hand a credit card. 'Ain't it amazing? No-one needs money anymore. You just carry one of these little pieces of plastic, and you can get *anything* you want! I just been told we can fly to Hawaii just by showing the right person this little card. It sure was a lucky day for us when we found this!'

They'd *found* it! The hotel room, drinks, steak sandwiches for the dog, margueritas had all been down to this credit card they'd found.

'Finish your beer, Luke, c'mon, let's go.' They whistled the dog, and off they went. Presumably to have another party in Hawaii.

It was the tour of America that got me thinking about a definite direction. I had always sung (in all the bands I'd been in) with an American accent. Nothing strange in that. All English pop bands did. I began to have this niggling feeling, though, that there was something not quite *real* about it. Now I didn't want to forsake the Rock 'n' Roll feel that I had, but at the same time I didn't want to be looked upon as a Rock 'n' Roll revivalist. There must be a way of keeping the feel, but singing in my own accent. About things *I* knew about. I tried writing a cockney song with Tony Colton for the 'Tracks' album, but it never really come off. We ended up using just the intro to it as an introduction to 'Hot Property'. But it was a start.

When I began working in the States, I realised that although that particular effort at a cockney song didn't really come off, the idea was right. When I got up in front of them American audiences singing things like 'Oh Mama, ya alraht,' and 'The boy cain't even daince', I felt such a fraud. It didn't seem so bad doing it in England. At home it sort of felt like you were giving 'em a taste of what you thought a good American band would sound like. But here we were, in America, showing 'em what a good *English* band sounded like. But we were singing in their accent!

Jerry Lee, Little Richard, Fats Domino sang in their own accents. That's why I liked 'em. They were *real*. It suddenly became plainly obvious. Everybody should sing in their own naturalised accent. Whether you're from Memphis, New York, Newcastle, Glasgow. It's what I've go to do.

I began changing a few words. I'd sing 'Oh Muvver' instead of 'Oh Mama'. Daft, I know, 'cos the lyrics didn't translate properly. But I felt better doing it. I began to feel a bit more real. All that needed to be done was to write a song thinking in my own accent. That's it! The idea became an obsession. I had found my direction.

It wouldn't be easy, but I had the feeling that it would work. I began making mental plans. But in the meantime, while I was in America, I was gonna enjoy myself. It was the Land of Music as far as I was concerned, and I wanted to see and hear as much of it as I could.

The tour was strenuous. A different place every night and, America being the size it is, we flew everywhere. We had to be up early most mornings to catch the plane to the next town. I vowed every morning (you know how I love mornings!) that after the gig that evening I'd get an early night. But that night we'd be somewhere like St Louis. For *one* night only! How can I go to bed knowing there's probably some fantastic band playing in some club just around the corner? I couldn't do it. We'd be gone next day. I'd get no second chance.

Me and Albert would ask around after the gig where the music was, and off we'd go. If we got to sit in with the band, which happened most times (we made sure of that), our night was complete. Or almost. We usually ended up in the guitar player's or the banjo player's hotel room, singing and strumming 'til it was time to catch the plane to the next town.

If we had any time off, and we did get one or two days, it was spent in LA. That was where we were based. There was *always* someone to see in LA. I went to see James Brown at the Forum. He was great. So was the black comedian on before him. The audience, mostly black, were falling about in the aisles. Their laughter was infectious. I was laughing with 'em. I couldn't help it, though I didn't understand a word he was on about!

A late night club in LA was the Palomino. It was a C & W club. I saw Doug Kershaw there. A wild fiddle-playing Cajun. I loved it. I was playing a bit of fiddle in the act with Heads Hands and Feet. We found out he was staying at our hotel and that night me and Smiffy (Ray Smith) had a fiddle-playing, guitar-strumming session in his room. I remember (just about!) writing a song with him. Though I can't recall the tune.

The next day we were playing at the Whiskey, and Doug Kershaw said he was coming down. That afternoon I got my fiddle out for a bit ofpractice. There was a knock on the door. I put my fiddle down on the bed and went to open it.

It was Smiffy. Now Smiffy was having the time of his life in America. He loved Hollywood, he loved the film stars, he loved Tequila Sunrises and he loved the girls. He was convinced that oysters kept him in shape. He had 'em for breakfast, dinner, tea and supper. Smiffy threw himself hook, line and sinker into whatever part he was playing.

The part he was now playing was 'The English Rock 'n' Roll Superstar'.

Not long after we arrived in the States he said to me, 'Someone told me, Charlie, that in America they spike your drinks with LSD and that.'

'I've heard that, too, Ray,' I said.

'Well,' said Ray, 'at that party the other night, I went round all of 'em and not one of 'em was spiked!'

I laughed, and so did Ray – but only after *I* laughed. He meant it!

Smiffy wrote great songs and was one of the nicest blokes you could ever meet. He was also one of the clumsiest.

John Wayne was his favourite actor and he loved Elvis and Stanley Matthews. He hit on this idea that he reckoned would improve his stage image. He was gonna stand and 'look about' like John Wayne, while using the legwork of Elvis and the footwork of Stanley Matthews. The result was fantastic!

'Ray,' I said, 'you've hit on a gimmick that someone like Jerry Lewis would give his right arm for.'

'Jerry Lewis? Don't you mean Jerry *Lee* Lewis?'

'No. Jerry Lewis. I love him, and what you just done was on a par with anything *he's* ever done.'

Ray dropped it. He hadn't meant for it to be funny. His new American image had to be Moody. They didn't know he was clumsy. They didn't know he was an ordinary bloke who liked a laugh. It was his big chance to put over the Ray Smith He Wanted To Be.

'Stars' had a reputation of being able to pull any bird they wished. Ray set to work. He decked himself out in velvet trousers and five-inch high-heel boots (which gave him a 'Here's me head, me arse in coming' walk) and away he went. He planned a line of chat that was unique. He'd swotted up on phrases that sounded deep and poetic (all nicked from somewhere or other). The idea was to let 'em loose when the timing was right. There he'd be, in the foyer of the Continental Hyatt House, LA (the groupies' paradise, and Smiffy's) looking about, all John Wayne cool.

'Hey! Aren't you with that new English Rock Band?' A dodgy bunch of groupies had homed in on Ray. They needed an 'in'. Someone to get 'em past the doorman. 'Yeh!' That was enough. No questions about 'What new English Rock Band?' in case it was the wrong one. 'Care to join me for dinner, girls?'

Smiffy was there! At the dinner table surrounded by admiring birds! Weyheyyy!! Long live Elvis and John Wayne and Hollywood and America and . . . but hang about . . . don't go too mad yet. Play it cool, Smiffy boy. Ray goes into a theatrical pose and gazes into the distance. It was time for his pulling plan to be pulled out of the bag. Smiffy had set up a pregnant pause and was about to give birth.

'Far be it for me to gander into a ladies' chamber, but sail on silver silver!'

A sort of mixture of Shakespeare and Simon and Garfunkel.

It worked! The one he fancied was impressed.

'Hey, Ray, did that just come straight off the top of your head?'

'Pardon, Mam? Oh yeh, I'm sorry, just thinking out loud.'

'That was great! It sounded like a line out of a great song. Couldn't you use it?'

'Well, it could be tidied up a little. Hey waiter! Tequila Sunrises all round and a plate of oysters.'

Ray was away! What could possibly go wrong? But it was Smiffy playing a part. You knew sooner or later the *real* Smiffy was gonna reveal himself. Looking her straight in the eyes he's gone:

'How about making it with me down to the gig tonight? Ahh! Here's the drinks. Thanks, waiter. Here, keep the change.'

'But it's a 100-dollar bill, sir.'

'Is it not enough?'

'More than enough, Sir!'

'Keep it!' says Ray, and with a smile and a sweep of his arm, meant to convey to the waiter that money means nothing, manages to sweep the drinks, trays of hamburger relish, tomato ketchup and anything else that was in his path, off the table and all over the birds.

The *real* Smiffy had arrived, bless him!

Ray's got up. 'You alright, love?' Trying to brush off tomato ketchup from some tart's dress with a dirty hanky he's just pulled out of his pocket. 'I'm sorry, love, let me . . .' But it was too late. They were all up now, backing away from Smiffy. Smiffy blew his nose, which he did continually as the *real* Smiffy, leaving tomato ketchup on the end. 'Girls! Do you still think any of you might be still coming to the gig tonight?'

They were gone. To the powder room to get cleaned up. The odds were they weren't coming back. Not to Smiffy's table anyway. Smiffy's sat there with a furrowed forehead. But only for a minute.

'Charlie!' He's spotted me across the restaurant. 'Charlie! Weyheyy!' His big Smiffy grin taking over. 'Where's Albert? Are we going clubbing it tonight after the gig, or what? There's a Country and Western club just off the Strip. We'll take our guitars. I got this new tuning worked out. Let's go to the bar, I want to tell you about it.'

We go to the bar. 'Ray, you've got tomato ketchup on your nose.' 'Where?' He gets his hanky out. 'Is it gone?' 'Yeh.' Smiffy stuffs his hanky back in his pocket. The bit of ketchup is now on his moustache. 'What I was thinking was, if you tune your G down to F and your D down to D flat . . .'

Well, this was Smiffy. Now you've got the picture I'll goback to what I was telling you. I *bet* you guess what happens. I'll recap. There was me sitting on the bed practising my fiddle, hear knock on door, lay fiddle down, open door. It was Smiffy.

But just to be fair, I wanna get across to you that what was about to happen was entirely *my* fault. Although Smiffy did it. Now, if you've got a dog that you know likes chewing your boots up, well you don't leave 'em about, do you? You put 'em away, out of his reach. Also , if you've got kids that are in the toddling stage, then you don't deck out your house with breakables that they can get their hands on? If you do and they break 'em, or you do and your boots get chewed up, it's *your* fault. I know what dogs are like. I know what kids are like. I wouldn't want 'em any other way. I knew what Smiffy was like, and I wouldn't want him any other way. But as soon as I saw his face at the door, I should have

Fiddlin' days. H H & F, 1971.

Heads Hands & Feet. Pete Gavin, Ray Smith, Albert Lee, me, Mike O'Neil and, standing at the back, Tony Colton.

reacted instantly. It was only the difference of a fraction of a second. But it was long enough for Ray to get past me and into my room.

'Ray! Don't sit . . .' Too late. 'CRACK!!!' You've guessed, ain't you? It don't take much figuring out. I was gonna say, 'Ray, don't sit down onthe bed.' It don't matter though, I shouldn't have left it there. Ray knew what he had done, but he didn't move. He just sat there. He didn't want to get up and *see* it. He just looked up at me with a 'Done it again' expression on his face.

'Get up, Ray,' I said quietly. 'Let's have a look.'

Ray got up. Still not looking.

There it lay and, surprisingly enough, it didn't look as bad as I thought.

'It don't look too bad, Ray.' But I knew I was kidding myself. I'd heard that 'CRACK!!!'

'It's alright, Charlie,' said Ray, making a grab for it.

'Don't touch it!' I panicked, 'leave it to me, Ray!'

The angle of the fiddle's fingerboard in relation to the body didn't look quite right. I picked it up. The only thing that joined the top bit to the bottom bit was four slack strings.

He'd broke the fuckin' neck off.

'I'll get it fixed for you, Charlie.'

'Ray, we're on stage in an hour.'

'I'll get one, don't worry.'

He was gone and back in five minutes.

'I've just bin up to Doug Kershaw's room. He said he'll lend you his.'

It was a nice thought and I was tempted, but the thought of Smiffy treading on Doug Kershaw's fiddle brought me out in a cold sweat.

'No, Ray, we'll have to get one from somewhere else.'

We hired one and the gig went off okay. Doug Kershaw turned up and was impressed. Smiffy was happy. 'Weyheyy, Charlie!!'

All's well that ends well. Smiffy got mine fixed next day. Bless him again!

Chapter 18

HH & F — RIP

Back home in England we carried on gigging, but I was becoming increasingly dissatisfied with what I was doing. I appreciated that it was a great band in a lot of people's eyes, but it still wasn't *my* ideal band.

I was ready for the change, but I suppose I was waiting for the right opportunity. I began playing from the head rather than the heart. It was interesting but the buzz was different. The heart *must* come first. The head works out all manner of things but as long as it knows that the heart is the governor, it can't go wrong. Festivals began to be the most coveted gigs. You could get across to thousands in just one performance. It would take at least a dozen normal gigs to cover the same amount of ground as one festival gig. I weighed it up in my head. It made sense, but after doing a few I wrote a poem. From the heart.

FESTIVALS

Now Rock 'n' Roll Festivals might seem exciting events,
But don't ever play on 'em, if you've got any sense.
I've bin in a few bands and done gigs big and small,
But them Festivals, well, they're the worst of 'em all.
Thousands of people all acting the cunt,
'Specially the ones who stand round the front.
Shovin' their heads in the PA stacks,
It's a wonder they don't all have heart attacks.
I should be excited, but I ain't, 'cos you see,
I'm afraid it's a load of old bollocks to me.
But I accepted the gig and I'm doin' me best
To gee meself up, though I'm far from impressed.
'Not long to go now,' I'm starting to think,
'I'll soon be back in the caravan, having a drink.'
Then the singer starts jumpin' all over the stage,m
He's suddenly gone mad, like he's bin let out of a cage.
Then some fat geezer (who's runnin' the show)
Shouts out, 'You've got one more number to go!'
'Fank Christ!' you say, 'cos it's startin' to rain,
And you wish you was back in them clubs again.
Then your amp packs up 'cos the rain's got in it,
So you shout for the Roady, he says, 'Hang on a minute!'
Then the Roady comes on and gives it a thump,
And I think to meself, 'Oh well, *he's* got the hump!'
'It's knackered,' he says. Well, what a brilliant observation!
'I'll get you a lead from the 'lectric Ovation.'
'That's no good!' I shout. 'It's me AMP that's gone!'
But he ain't took no notice. For Christ's sake, COME ON!
HURRY UP! I'm nearly comin' up to me solo!'

Meanwhile the stage is more suitable for playin' water polo.
Then me Amp gets wet and sparks start to fly,
And I think, 'Any minute we're all gonna die.'
I holler to the Roady, 'Hurry up! 'Fore it blows!'
But the Roady's too busy stuffin' something up his nose.
Now the singer's gone spare, all shakin' his head.
He don't even notice me amp's gone dead.
He's decided he's gonna start climbin' about.
He's climbed up on the PA and starts to shout out,
He's stood there, balanced on this little shelf,
He don't know he's makin' a cunt of hisself.
Get 'em all clappin', that's his philosophy,
But I'm afraid it's a load of old bollocks to me.
He shouts to the crowd, 'Can you hear me out there?'
'All clap your hands and all shout "OH YEH!"'
Though the rain's pourin' down and the wind is a-blowin',
The front man's determined to get 'em all goin',
He's jumped down and starts sliding all over the deck,
And I think any minute now he's gonna break his fuckin' neck.
Then he spins round and I think, 'Oh no, here he comes!'
And he picks up a stick and starts banging the drums.
The drummer gets humpy and shouts, 'Leave 'em alone!'
But the ol' front man's in a world of his own.
Then the fat geezer (the one who's runnin' the show)
Shouts, 'COME ON, GET OFF, WE'VE GOT 10 GROUPS TO GO!'
Then we all go mad, and all jump about,
And we hit the last chord with an almighty clout.
Then we run from the stage to get out of the rain,
And I'm thinking, 'I must be outa me brain!'
Then the singer says, 'WE had 'em goin' in the end!'
I nod, but then, oh well, let him pretend.
Cos' the crowd, they just sat there as quiet as can be,
While I thought, 'It's a load of old bollocks to me!'

Well, take from it what you will. It's basically true. My summary of all the festivals I've ever done. But it's all experience ain't it?

Heads Hands and Feet were getting a name, but we weren't getting in the Charts. It was decided that we needed a single. We did one. It was a good one too, as far as singles go. I got credit for a share in the writing. My only contribution was telling Ray and Tony the bits I liked and the bits I didn't like. The bits I liked they kept in, and the bits I didn't like were dropped. Not enough in my book to be credited with part of the writing, but, nevertheless, full credit to Ray and Tony, they gave me part of the song. I found out later, though, that although I felt I didn't deserve it, my contribution was a lot more than some famous 'writers' had done. If ever I saw one name under a song title, to me it was obvious. *He* wrote it. Two names? Okay, one wrote the tune and the other the lyrics. Three names? A bit more difficult. Possibly the third helped with lyrics and tune. Not being experienced in songwriting, this is how I thought it went.

Perhaps it does in some cases. But sometimes I'd see a song credited to three or more writers. How the fuck did this work? Oh, yes. They all wrote a bit each. But no. I found out that a lot of my favourite songs were 'written' thus . . .

For example, a song is credited to six people.

First person actually wrote the song. All of it.
Second person was a publisher whose only part was to get the song to the artist.
Third person was a publisher's partner who had to have a bit if his mate got a bit. (This is a fact, even though it sounds daft.)
Fourth person was the artist whose part in writing the song was singing it. (If he didn't want to *sing* it, the song never got recorded.)
Fifth person was a producer. (I mean, he *did* get a commercial sound on the record. His normal percentage hardly pays for the petrol in his fleet of Rollers.)
Sixth person was the DJ. (I mean, how the people gonna hear it if he don't *play* it!)

On top of that, the actual percentages had to be negotiated sensibly. The Writer only *wrote* the song. Who the fuck knows him? They know the publisher (had many hits), they know the artist (had many hits), they know the producer (had many hits), they know the DJ (plugs all the hits). The songwriter? Well, who's heard of him? We might do soon, but we're giving him a *chance*. Let's grab the bunce while we can! Before he cottons onto our little game. Give him 5%, that leaves us 95%. Five into 95 goes nicely. Exactly 19% each.

This sort of thing went on. Probably still does. But it didn't go on with HH & F. I was given part of the writing royalties simply because I genuinely helped with the *song*. I appreciated that. But I still felt I didn't merit it.

The song I'm talking about was 'Warming Up The Band'. It didn't do what we hoped it would. It got the plays and everybody said, 'Why ain't this record a hit?' But it wasn't. The *people* just didn't buy it. They all liked it, sure, but they didn't buy it.

'I like your new record,' is often said to me and Dave. Great. But the test is to ask, 'Have you bought it?' 'Yes' was the general answer to 'No Pleasing You'. 'No' was the general answer to 'Miserable Saturday Night' and 'Poor Ol' Mr Woogie'.

You know where you are with people.

The people didn't buy 'Warming Up The Band'. Everybody said it *should* have been a hit, but it wasn't and that was that.

Things began to go wrong. Reasons why the band weren't making it were put forward. Now that the band were on the verge of making it, more and more people began slinging their oar in. The same people who, at the beginning, took no notice.

Somehow or other, Danny Secunda, the manager, got aimed out. The man who got the band off the ground. Who had faith when no-one else did. The band, instead of being a unit, began to be, once more, just a bunch of talented musicians with no leader and therefore no positive goal.

Unrest began to settle in the camp.

It's the same with any team of people who make up a unit. A band, a football team. The talent may be there, but they need a figurehead to be the boss. A father figure. Perhaps it's instinct. It's like a family. You all work together, but you know Dad is the Governor at the end of the day. How many times have you seen a football team fall by the wayside because they've lost their

Chas and Dave get together. This picture shows that our wives, Joan and Sue, were as enthusiastic as we were for the partnership to succeed.

manager to another team? They are still the same bunch of geezers, but they've lost a leader. Someone to work *for*. Like a dad. They may not always agree with their manager (like sometimes you might not agree with your Dad), but you respect him and inwardly feel that at the end of the day he is always right. A bunch of talented footballers or musicians can play well, but they need that extra push when under pressure. A good manager gives this, but Danny Secunda got aimed out and Reggy Lock took over.

Reggy Lock began acting as manager under Tony Colton's direction. No doubt this suited Tony. But he was also the singer, the songwriter and the producer of the band. Reggy suited him perfectly. He acted out TC's orders. Just like the Board of a football club who try to run their team through the manager. It might sound good in theory, but it don't work.

The band had lost its figurehead. Someone who would be impressed by, and work creatively with, the band product. Putting forward constructive criticism now and again, knowing from the heart what the band has got and only wanting the best out of them.

I began to lose interest. I liked Reggy Lock, but as a tour manager. Not a band manager. Tony Colton has talent but he wanted to do too much. A great songwriter and a great producer but he should have stopped there.

Me and Albert started making plans for a new band. One more album was made with Heads Hands and Feet, 'Old Soldiers Will Never Die', but me and Albert had decided. We wanted to leave and form our own band.

We announced our decision.

It was to be the band we'd often talked about. Me and Albert were really close in our likes and dislikes in music. I was enthusiastic. I wanted to get a band going. I wasn't interested in the fame and glory, I just wanted to be part of my ideal band. So did Albert. But the record company thought different. I don't know why I didn't see it at the time. But now I do. I was blinded by my love of music. The record company saw Albert as the new guitar hero. As long as he was up front making a guitar noise, they saw money. They weren't interested in the type of music we were gonna play.

The new band was formed, but it never felt right from the start. From the off we wanted it to have a new name, but the record company talked us into calling it The New Head Hands and Feet. The line-up was me, Albert, Dave Peacock, Ian Wallace and Steve Simpson. All good players. But it was a rehash. We did a few gigs and went down alright but there was no real spirit there. The record company was pushing Albert up the front which he didn't really want. They were turning up on gigs, reporting back on the 'goods' and the 'bads' on everything we did. Fuck it! Here we go again. This is not how we meant it to be. What happened to the *band* we'd talked about? We wanted to *play* again and not be judged on 'Hit Potential'. We had more to offer than that. But I felt that it would be, in the end, up to us and I was willing to give it a real go. If it didn't work, then it wouldn't be for want of trying. But it never got that far. One night, three or four weeks after the new band had formed, me, Dave and Albert went for a drink down the Speakeasy. The Crickets were playing. They asked Albert to join 'em and he did.

I don't blame Albert. It was what he wanted to do. I admit I was choked at the time. All them months we'd talked about our 'Ideal Band' together. Now I

The family as we were in 1974. Baby Nick, me, Joan, Kate and Juliet.

knew it was never going to be.

But ain't it strange how things work out? Or is it?

I remember my Mum saying, 'If you bank your hopes on anything in life and it don't work out, don't sit there grieving about it, get out and do the next best thing. Quite often you'll find that the next best thing turns out to be what you should have done in the first place.'

She was right.

The next best thing was getting together with my mate to form a duo called Chas and Dave.

THE END
(and the beginning)

INDEX

ACKNOWLEDGEMENT

Many thanks to the following for their help in providing illustrations for my book:
Ace Records, Tom Casey, Charly Records, Enfield Public Library and John Repsch.